Against the Wind

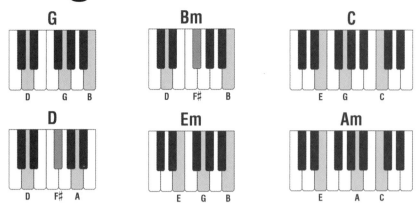

Words and Music by
Bob Seger

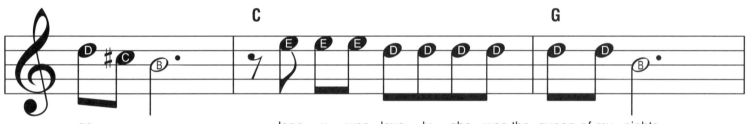

It seems like yes-ter-day, but it was long a-

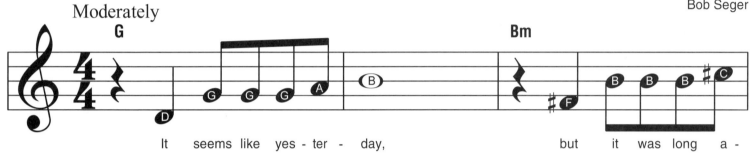

go. _____ Jane-y was love-ly, she was the queen of my nights,

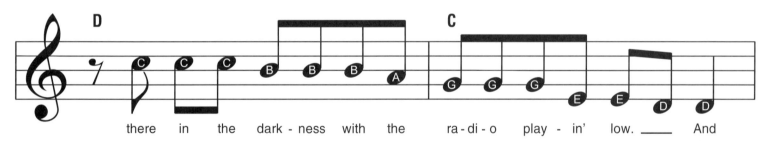

there in the dark-ness with the ra-di-o play-in' low. _____ And

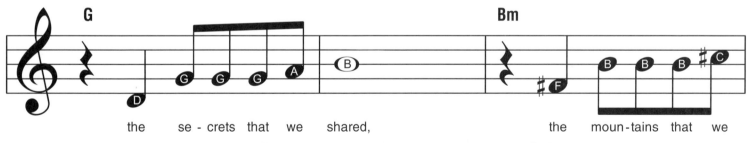

the se-crets that we shared, the moun-tains that we

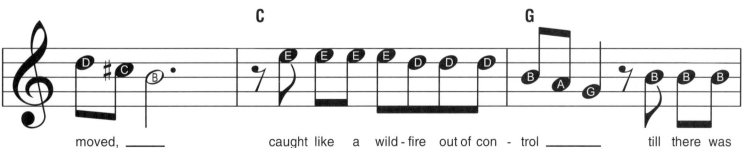

moved, _____ caught like a wild-fire out of con-trol _____ till there was

SUPER EASY SONGBOOK

CLASSIC ROCK

ISBN 978-1-5400-4316-0

HAL•LEONARD®

Visit Hal Leonard Online at
www.halleonard.com

Contact us:
Hal Leonard
7777 West Bluemound Road
Milwaukee, WI 53213
Email: info@halleonard.com

In Europe, contact:
Hal Leonard Europe Limited
42 Wigmore Street
Marylebone, London, W1U 2RN
Email: info@halleonardeurope.com

In Australia, contact:
Hal Leonard Australia Pty. Ltd.
4 Lentara Court
Cheltenham, Victoria, 3192 Australia
Email: info@halleonard.com.au

All Right Now

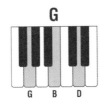
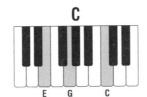
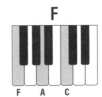

Words and Music by Andy Fraser
and Paul Rodgers

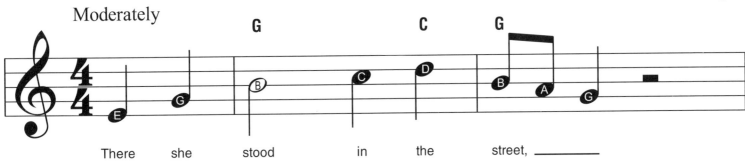

There she stood in the street, _____

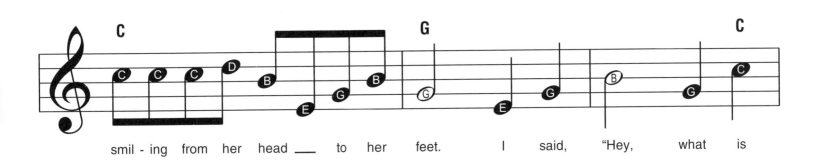

smil - ing from her head ___ to her feet. I said, "Hey, what is

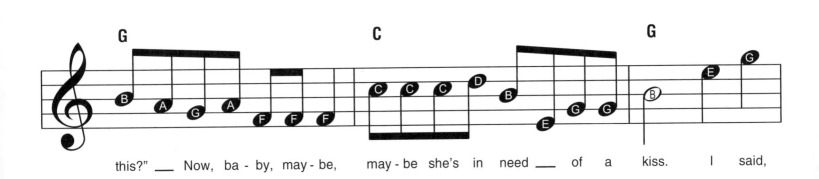

this?" ___ Now, ba - by, may - be, may - be she's in need ___ of a kiss. I said,

7

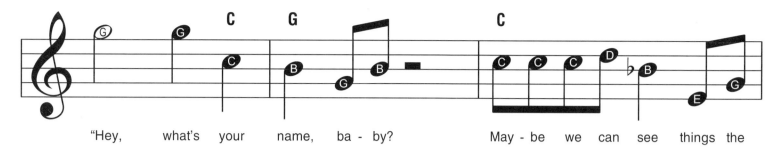

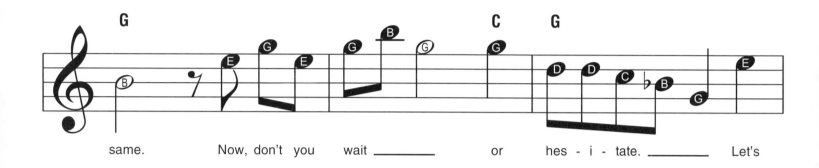

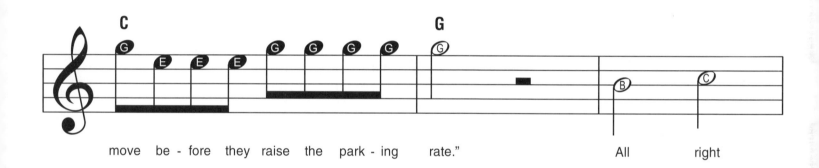

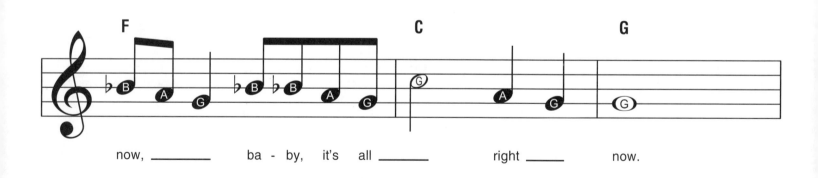

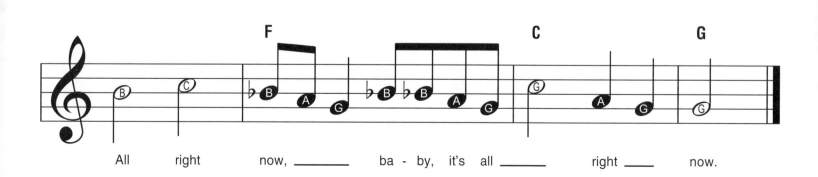

Already Gone

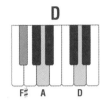
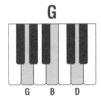
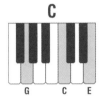

Words and Music by Jack Tempchin
and Robb Strandlund

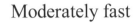

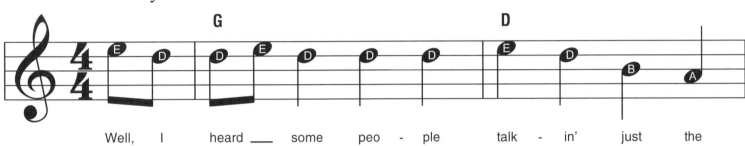

Well, I heard ___ some peo - ple talk - in' just the

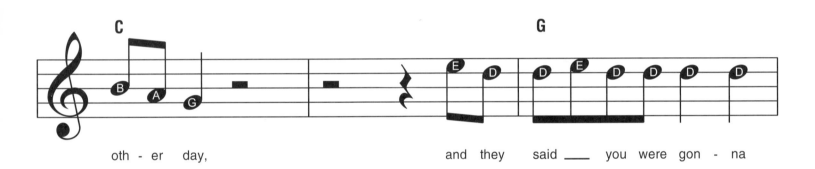

oth - er day, and they said ___ you were gon - na

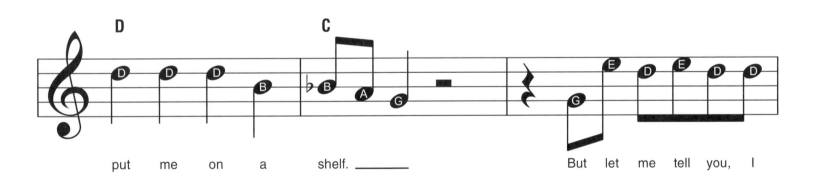

put me on a shelf. _____ But let me tell you, I

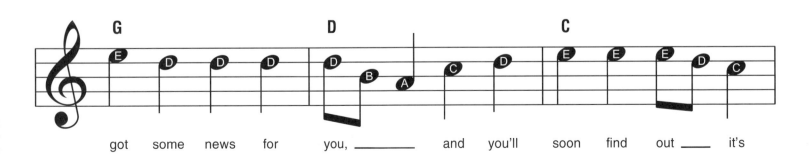

got some news for you, _____ and you'll soon find out ___ it's

true, and then you'll have ___ to eat your lunch all by your -

self. _____ 'Cause I'm al - read - y

gone. And I'm feel - in'

strong. ___ I will sing _____

_____ this vic - t'ry song. ___ 'Cause I'm

al - read - y gone.

American Girl

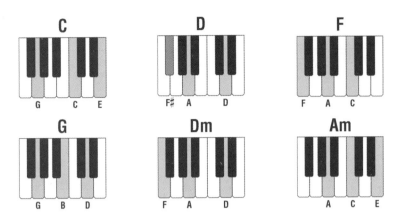

Words and Music by
Tom Petty

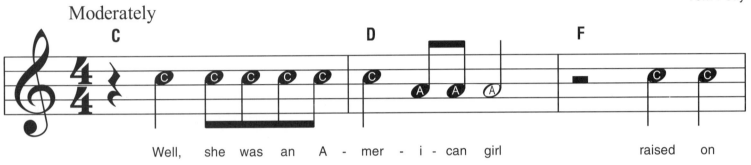

Well, she was an A - mer - i - can girl raised on

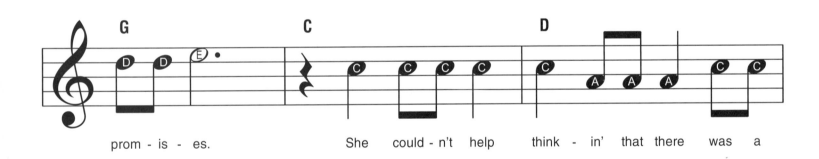

prom - is - es. She could - n't help think - in' that there was a

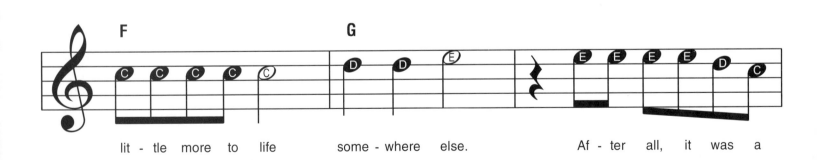

lit - tle more to life some - where else. Af - ter all, it was a

11

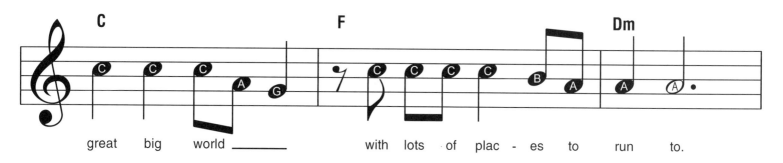

great big world _____ with lots of plac - es to run to.

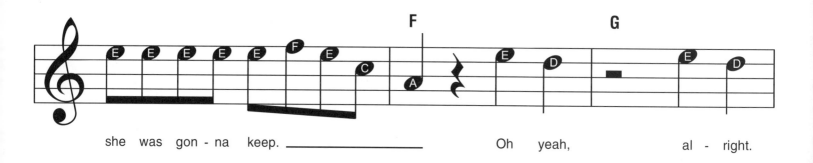

Yeah, and if she had to die try - in', she ___ had one lit-tle prom - ise

she was gon - na keep. _____ Oh yeah, al - right.

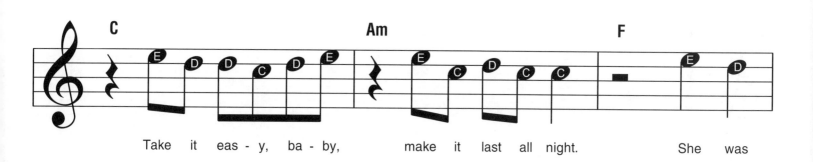

Take it eas - y, ba - by, make it last all night. She was

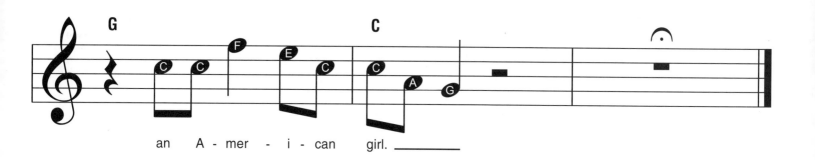

an A - mer - i - can girl. _____

Baba O'Riley

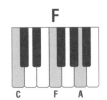
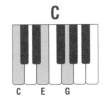
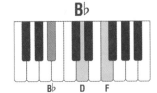

Words and Music by
Peter Townshend

Moderately

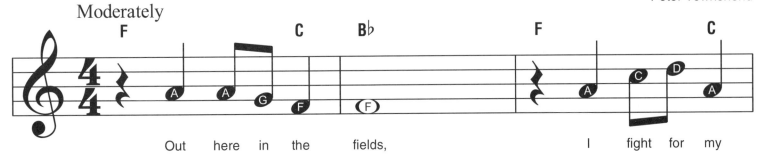

Out here in the fields, I fight for my

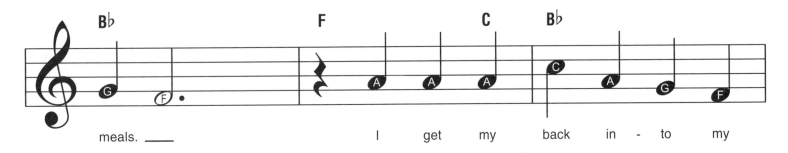

meals. ___ I get my back in - to my

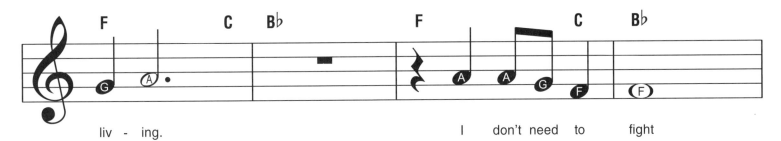

liv - ing. I don't need to fight

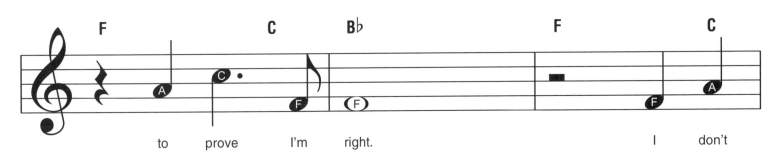

to prove I'm right. I don't

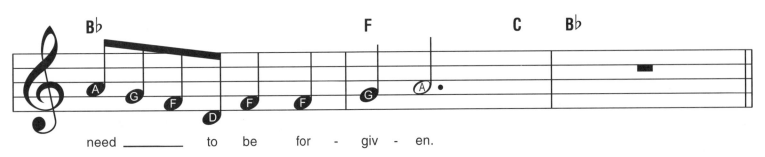

need ___ to be for - giv - en.

13

(Instrumental)

Don't cry, _____ don't raise your eye. _____

_____ It's on - ly teen - age waste - land. _____

_____ Teen - age waste - land, it's on - ly teen - age

waste - land. Teen - age waste - land,

teen - age waste - land.

Baby, I Love Your Way

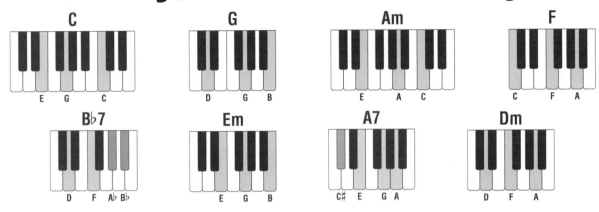

Words and Music by
Peter Frampton

Moderately

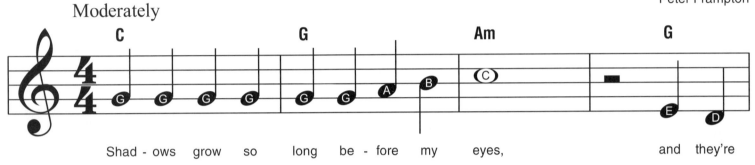

Shad-ows grow so long be-fore my eyes, and they're

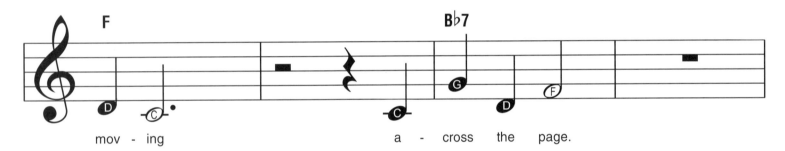

mov-ing a - cross the page.

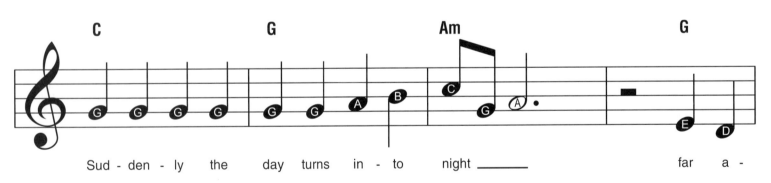

Sud-den-ly the day turns in-to night _____ far a-

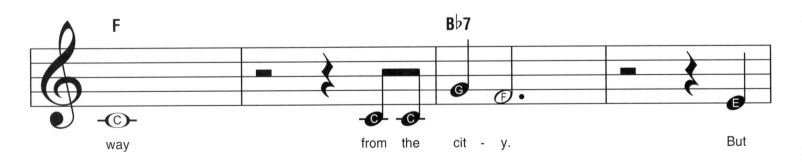

way from the cit-y. But

Beast of Burden

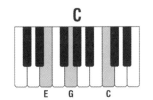
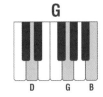
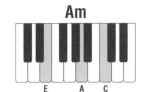
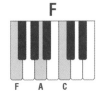

Words and Music by Mick Jagger
and Keith Richards

Moderate Rock

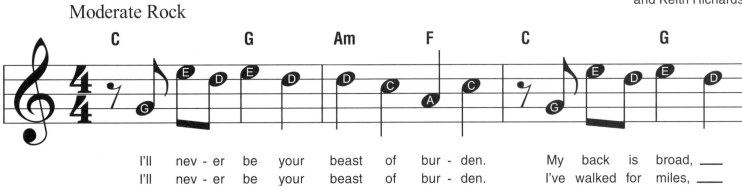

I'll nev-er be your beast of bur-den. My back is broad, ___
I'll nev-er be your beast of bur-den. I've walked for miles, ___

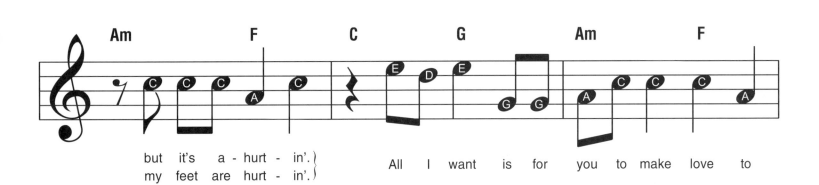

but it's a-hurt-in'.
my feet are hurt-in'.

All I want is for you to make love to

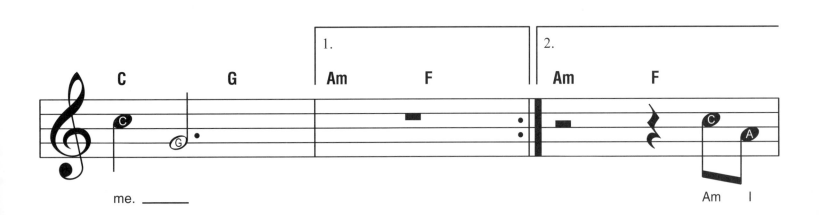

me. ___

Am I

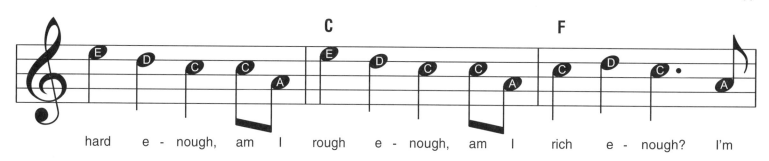

hard e - nough, am I rough e - nough, am I rich e - nough? I'm

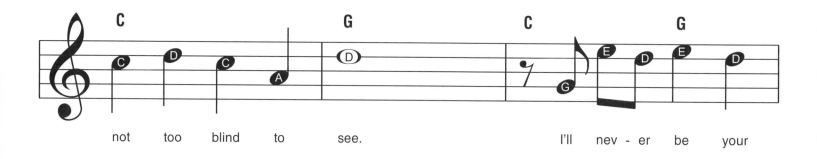

not too blind to see. I'll nev - er be your

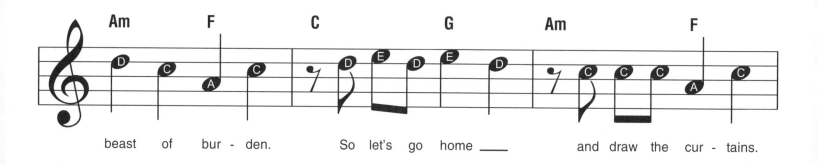

beast of bur - den. So let's go home ____ and draw the cur - tains.

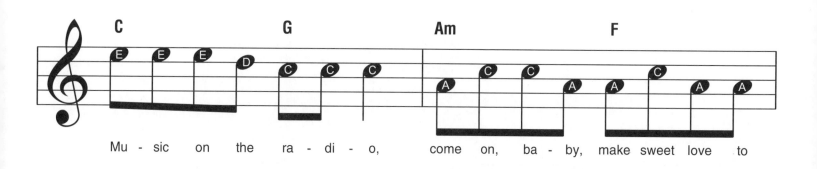

Mu - sic on the ra - di - o, come on, ba - by, make sweet love to

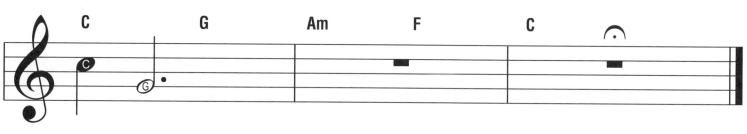

me. _____

Best of My Love

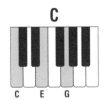
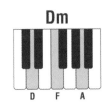
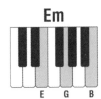
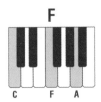
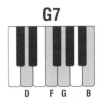

Words and Music by Don Henley,
Glenn Frey and John David Souther

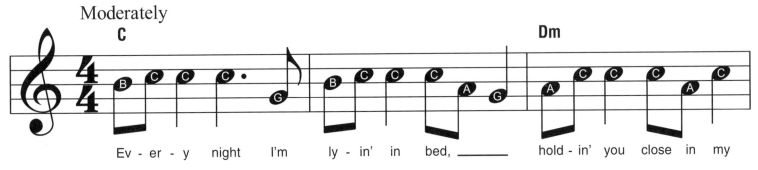

Ev - er - y night I'm ly - in' in bed, _____ hold - in' you close in my

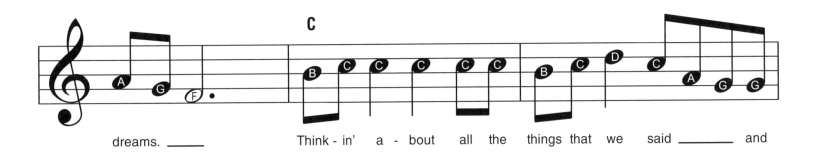

dreams. _____ Think - in' a - bout all the things that we said _____ and

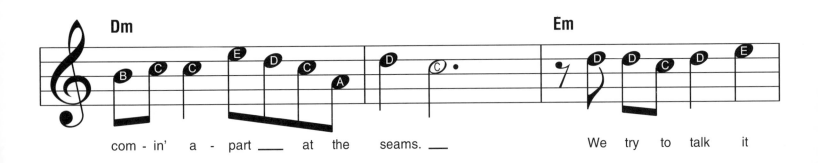

com - in' a - part _____ at the seams. _____ We try to talk it

19

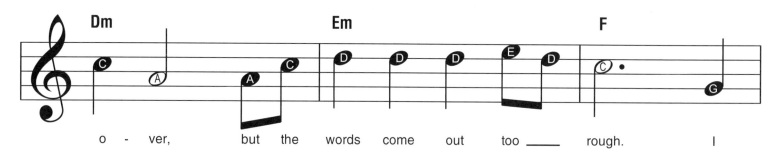

o - ver, but the words come out too ____ rough. I

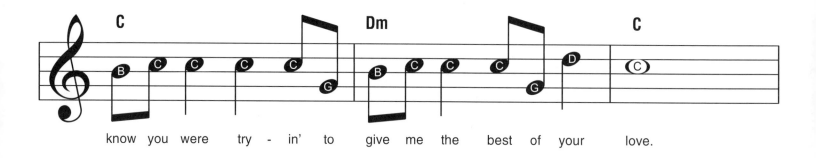

know you were try - in' to give me the best of your love.

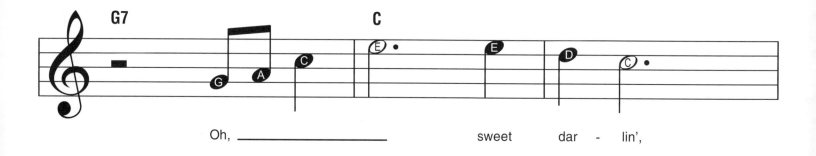

Oh, _____ sweet dar - lin',

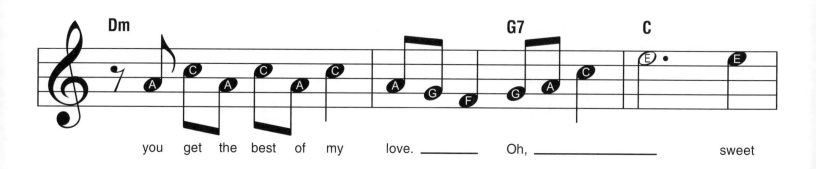

you get the best of my love. ____ Oh, _____ sweet

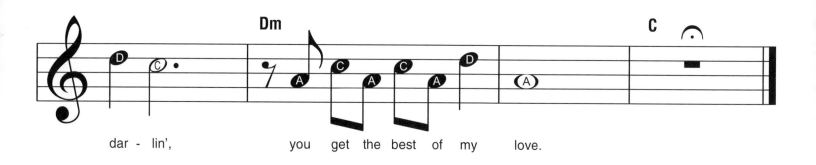

dar - lin', you get the best of my love.

Born to Be Wild

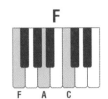
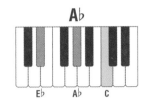
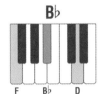

Words and Music by
Mars Bonfire

Moderately fast

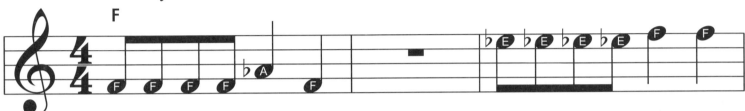

Get your mo - tor run - ning.   Head out on the high - way.

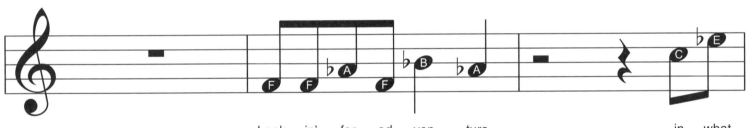

Look - in' for ad - ven - ture   in what -

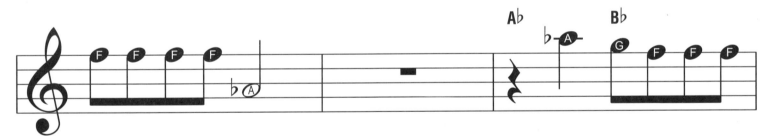

ev - er comes our way.   Yeah, dar - ling, gon - na

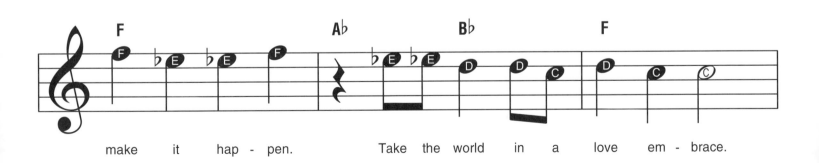

make it hap - pen. Take the world in a love em - brace.

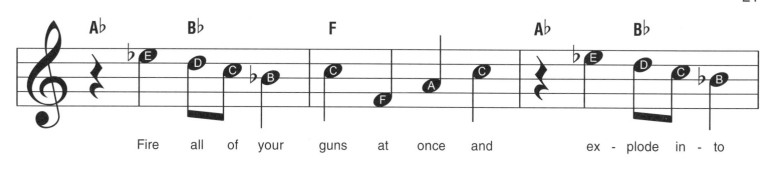

Fire all of your guns at once and ex - plode in - to

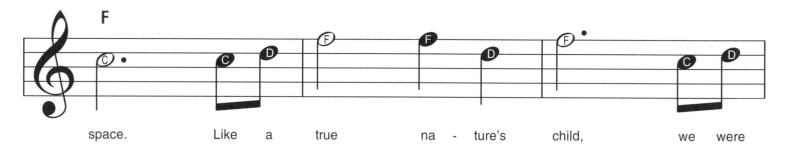

space. Like a true na - ture's child, we were

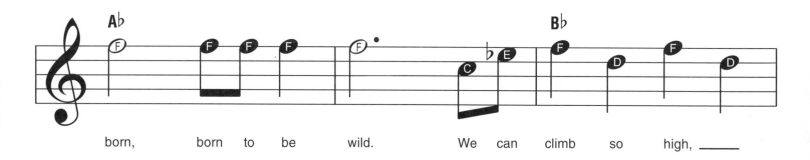

born, born to be wild. We can climb so high, _____

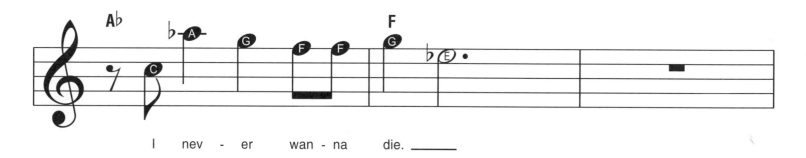

I nev - er wan - na die. _____

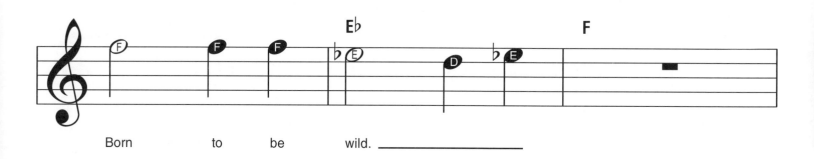

Born to be wild. _____

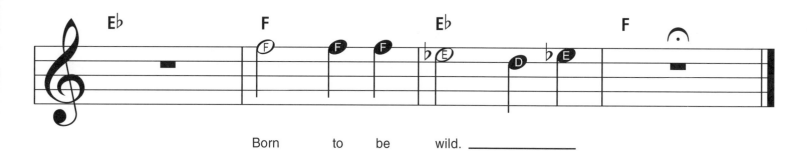

Born to be wild. _____

The Boys Are Back in Town

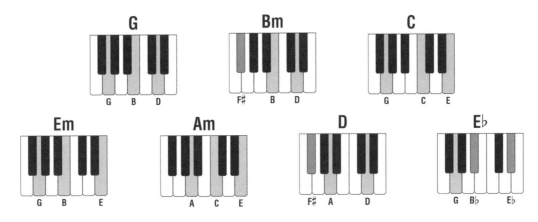

Words and Music by
Philip Parris Lynott

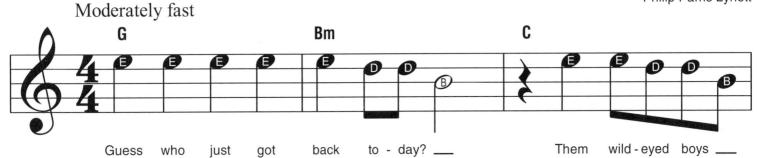

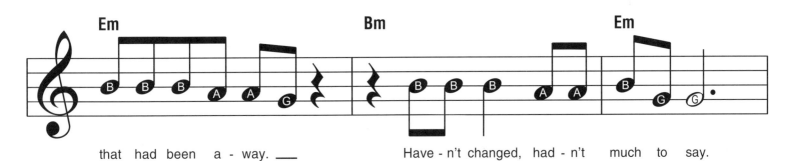

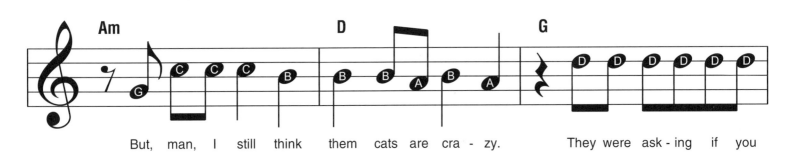

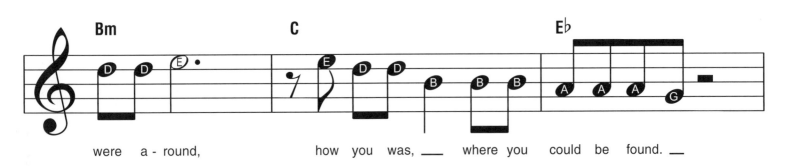

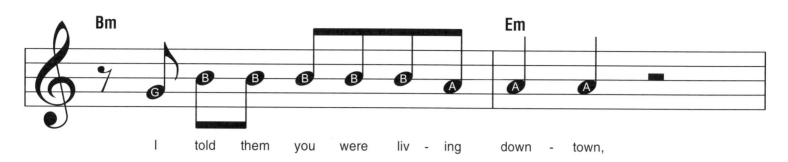

I told them you were liv - ing down - town,

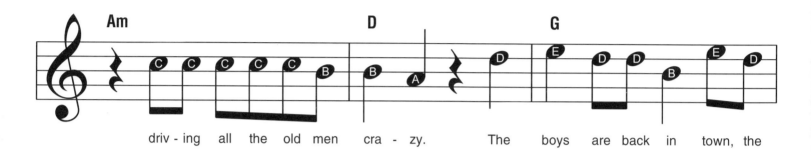

driv - ing all the old men cra - zy. The boys are back in town, the

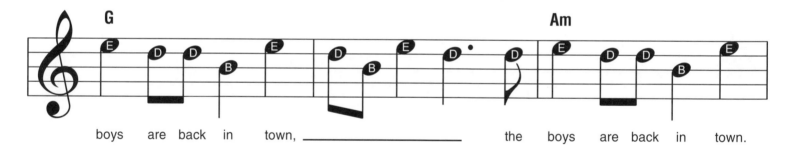

boys are back in town. I say, the

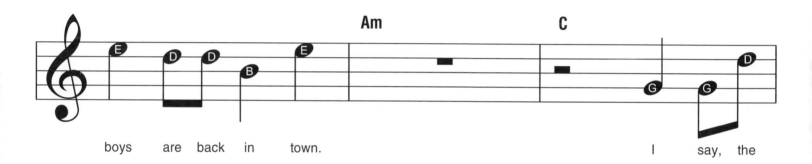

boys are back in town, _____ the boys are back in town.

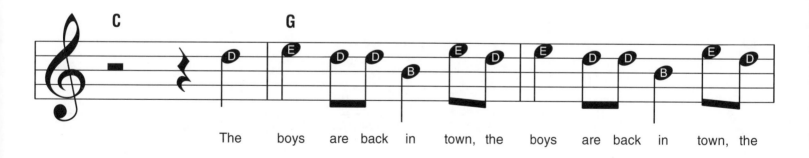

The boys are back in town, the boys are back in town, the

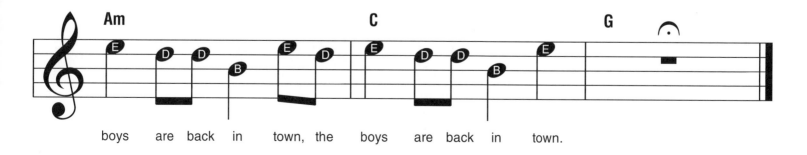

boys are back in town, the boys are back in town.

Call Me
from the Paramount Motion Picture AMERICAN GIGOLO

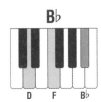
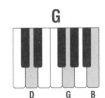
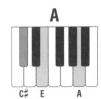
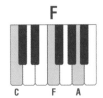

Words by Deborah Harry
Music by Giorgio Moroder

Moderately

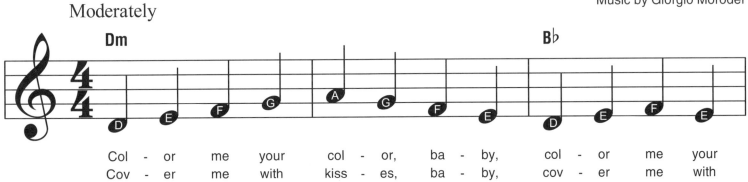

Col - or me your col - or, ba - by, col - or me your
Cov - er me with kiss - es, ba - by, cov - er me with

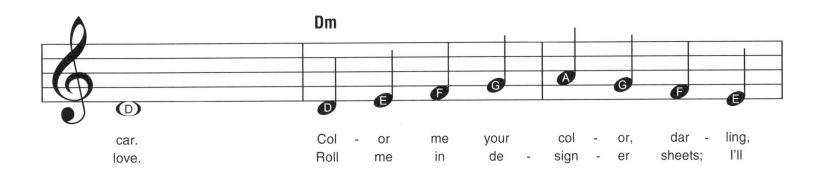

car. Col - or me your col - or, dar - ling,
love. Roll me in de - sign - er sheets; I'll

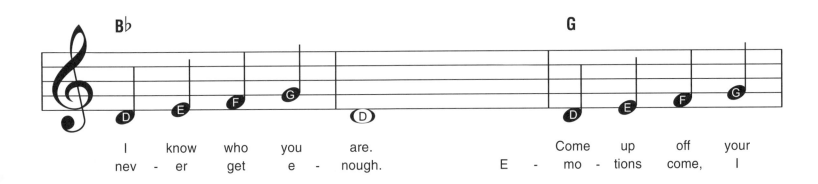

I know who you are. Come up off your
nev - er get e - nough. E - mo - tions come, I

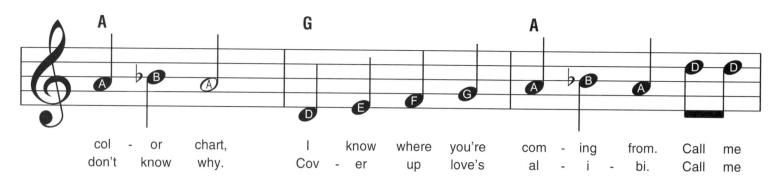

col - or chart, I know where you're com - ing from. Call me
don't know why. Cov - er up love's al - i - bi. Call me

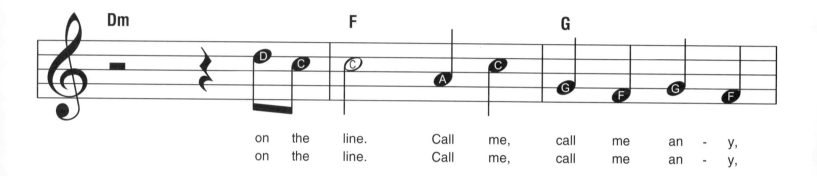

on the line. Call me, call me an - y,
on the line. Call me, call me an - y,

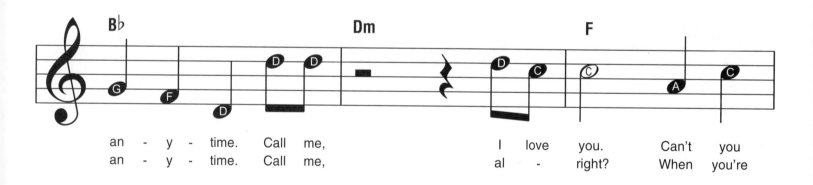

an - y - time. Call me, I love you. Can't you
an - y - time. Call me, al - right? When you're

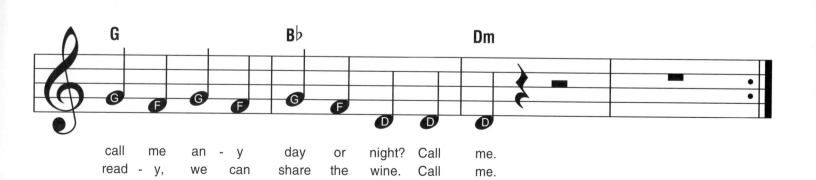

call me an - y day or night? Call me.
read - y, we can share the wine. Call me.

Carry On Wayward Son

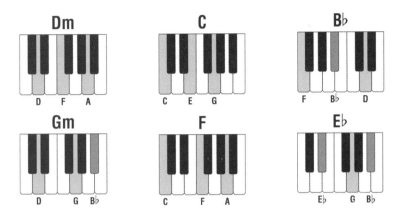

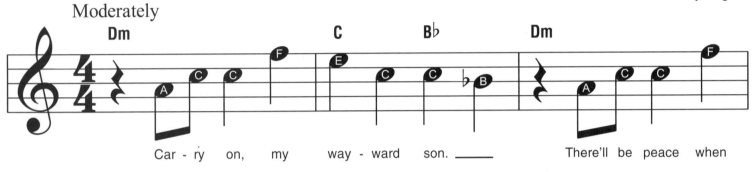

Words and Music by
Kerry Livgren

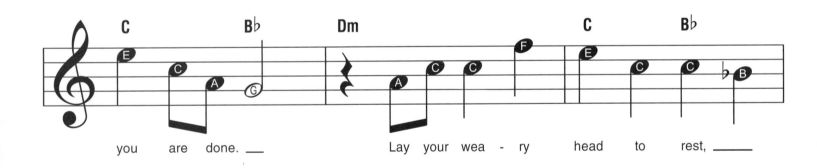

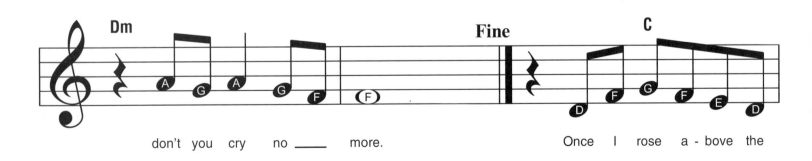

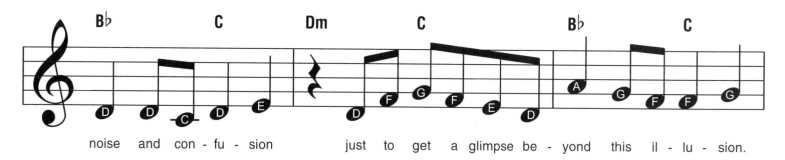

noise and con - fu - sion   just to get a glimpse be - yond this il - lu - sion.

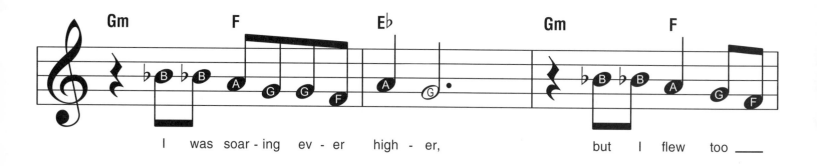

I was soar - ing ev - er high - er,   but I flew too ___

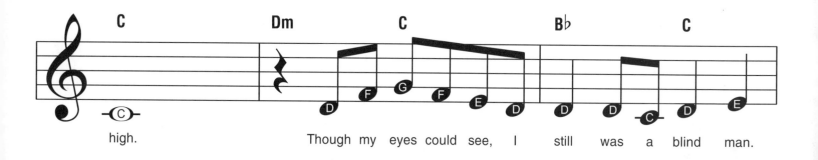

high.   Though my eyes could see, I still was a blind man.

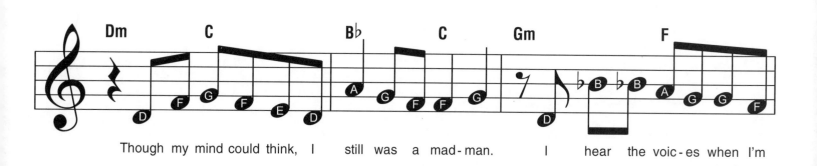

Though my mind could think, I still was a mad - man.   I hear the voic - es when I'm

D.C. al Fine
(Return to beginning
and play to Fine)

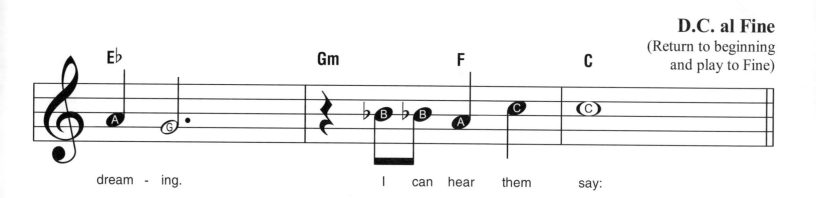

dream - ing.   I can hear them say:

China Grove

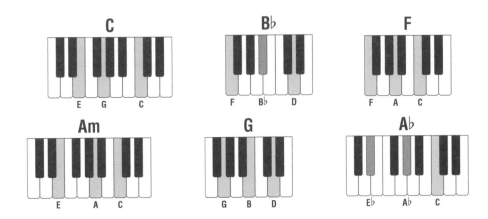

Words and Music by
Tom Johnston

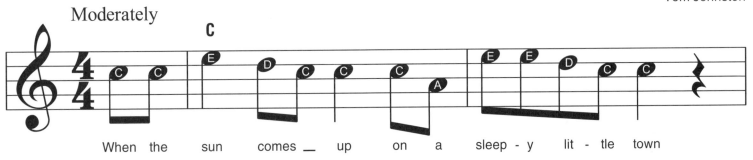

When the sun comes — up on a sleep-y lit-tle town

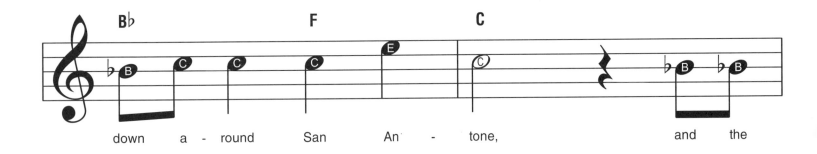

down a-round San An-tone, and the

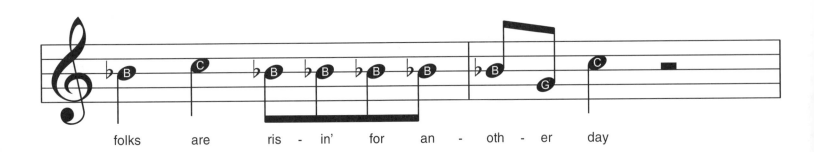

folks are ris-in' for an-oth-er day

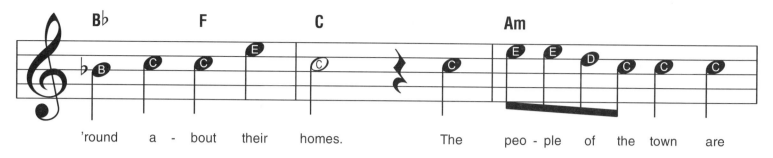

'round a - bout their homes. The peo - ple of the town are

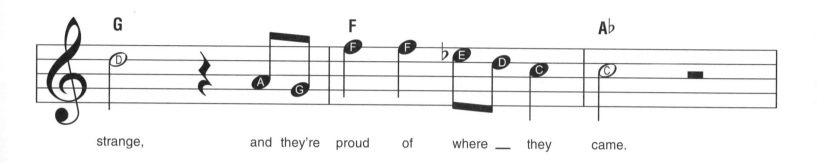

strange, and they're proud of where __ they came.

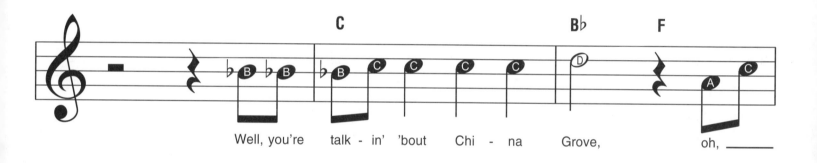

Well, you're talk - in' 'bout Chi - na Grove, oh, _____

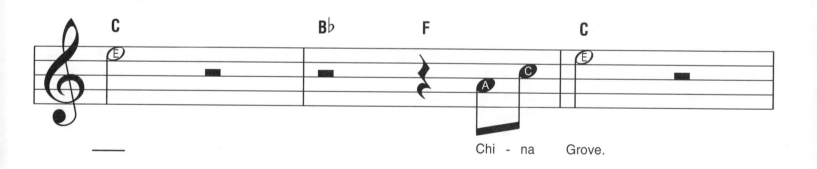

_____ Chi - na Grove.

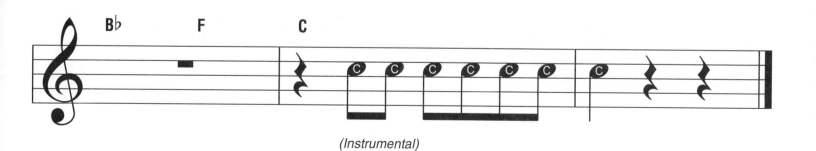

(Instrumental)

Come Sail Away

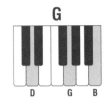
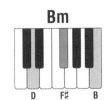
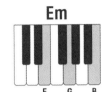
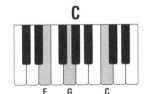
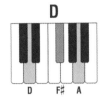

Words and Music by
Dennis DeYoung

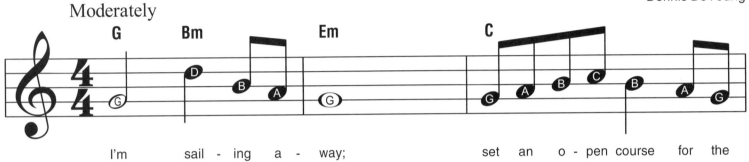

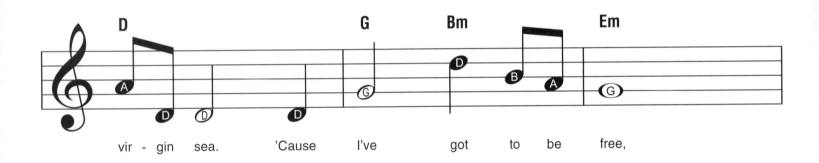

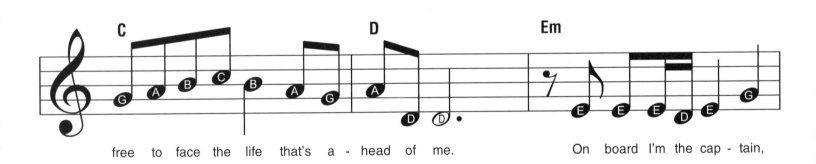

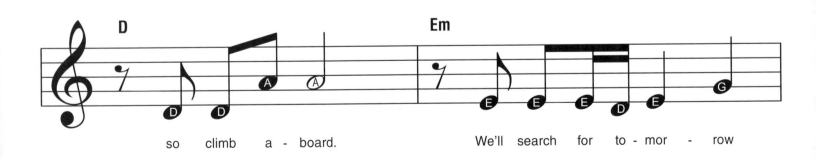

Crazy Little Thing Called Love

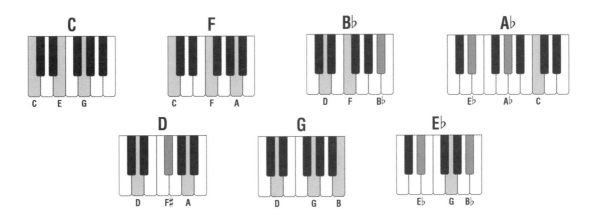

Words and Music by
Freddie Mercury

Moderately fast Shuffle

This thing called love, I just can't
thing called love, it just cries in a
cool, re-lax, get hip, get

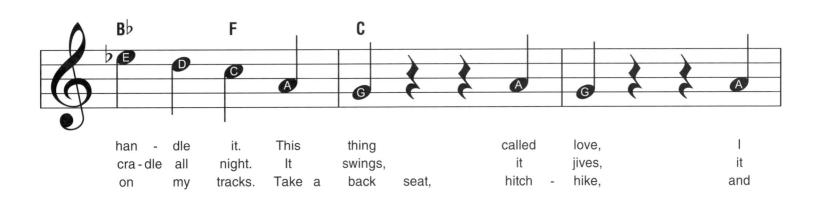

han-dle it. This thing called love, I
cra-dle all night. It thing swings, it jives, it
on my tracks. Take a back seat, hitch-hike, and

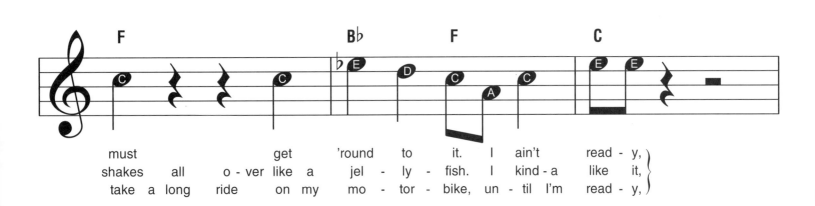

must get 'round to it. I ain't read-y,
shakes all o-ver like a jel-ly-fish. I kind-a like it,
take a long ride on my mo-tor-bike, un-til I'm read-y,

Don't Fear the Reaper

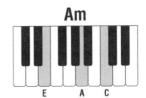
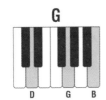
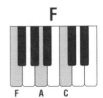
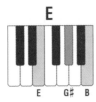

Words and Music by
Donald Roeser

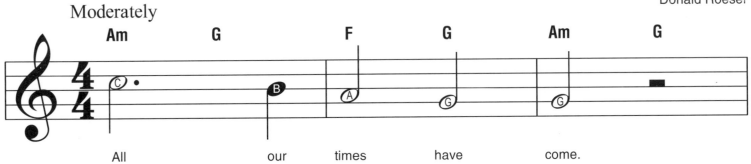

All our times have come.

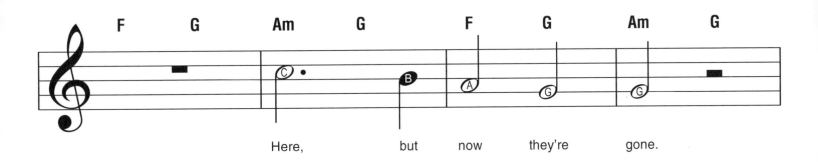

Here, but now they're gone.

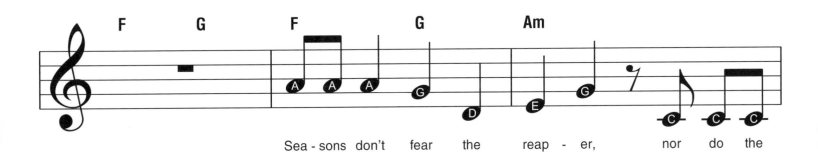

Sea - sons don't fear the reap - er, nor do the

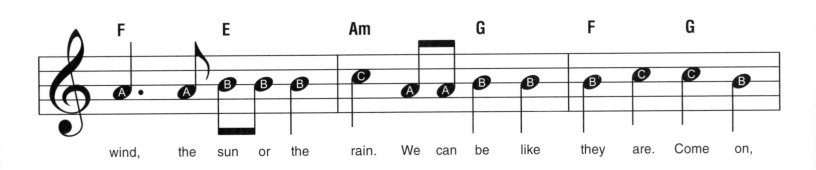

wind, the sun or the rain. We can be like they are. Come on,

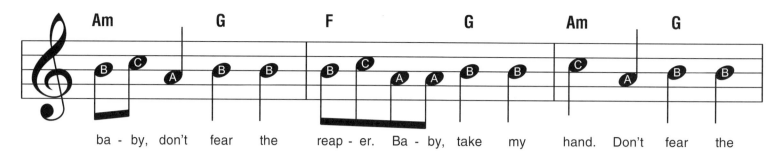

ba - by, don't fear the reap - er. Ba - by, take my hand. Don't fear the

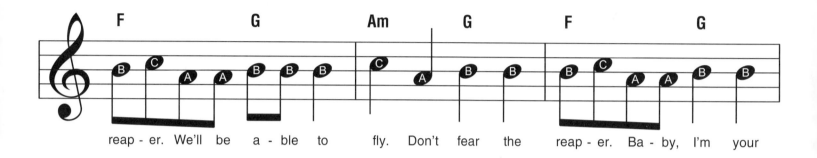

reap - er. We'll be a - ble to fly. Don't fear the reap - er. Ba - by, I'm your

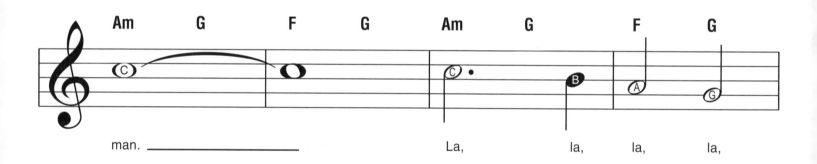

man. _____ La, la, la, la,

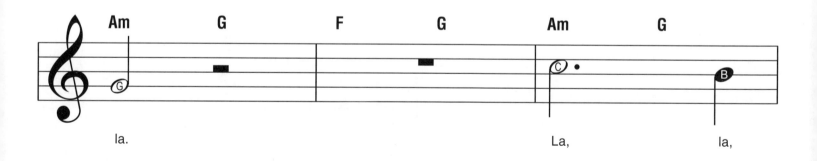

la. La, la,

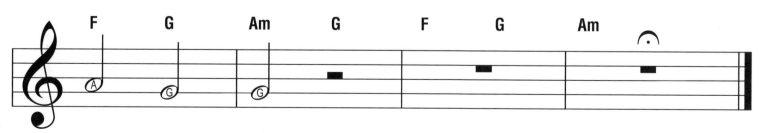

la, la, la.

Don't Stop Believin'

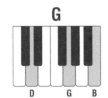
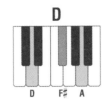
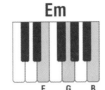
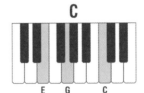
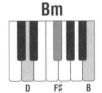

Words and Music by Steve Perry,
Neal Schon and Jonathan Cain

Just a small - town girl, liv - in' in a
Just a cit - y boy, born and raised in

lone - ly world. _____ She took the mid - night train go - in'
south De - troit. _____ He took the mid - night train go - in'

an - y - where. A sing - er in a
an - y - where.

smok - y room, the smell of wine and cheap per - fume. _____

For a smile ___ they can share the night. It goes on and on and

37

Down on the Corner

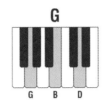
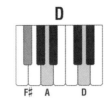
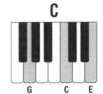

Words and Music by
John Fogerty

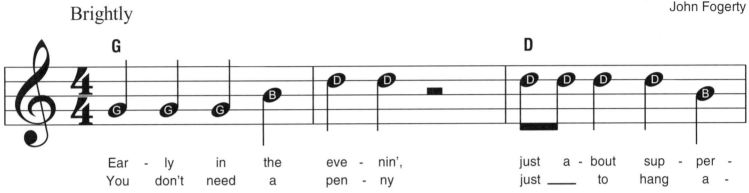

Ear - ly in the eve - nin', just a - bout sup - per -
You don't need a pen - ny just ___ to hang a -

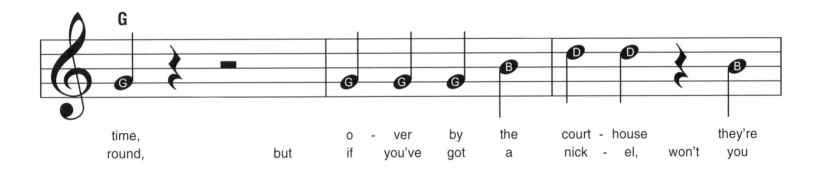

time, o - ver by the court - house they're
round, but if you've got a nick - el, won't you

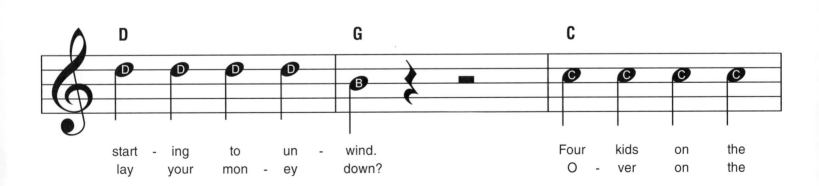

start - ing to un - wind. Four kids on the
lay your mon - ey down? O - ver on the

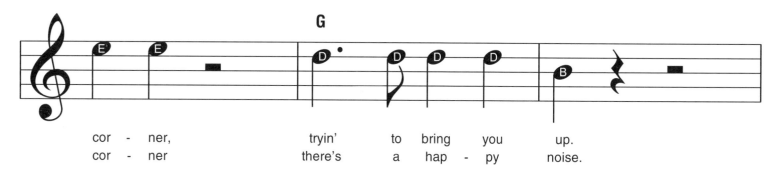

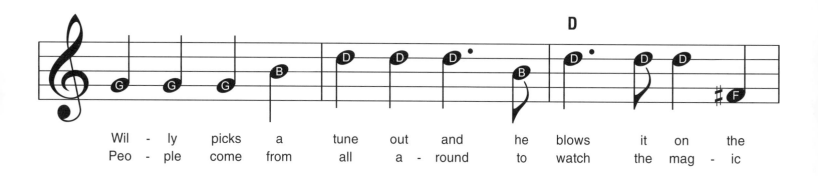

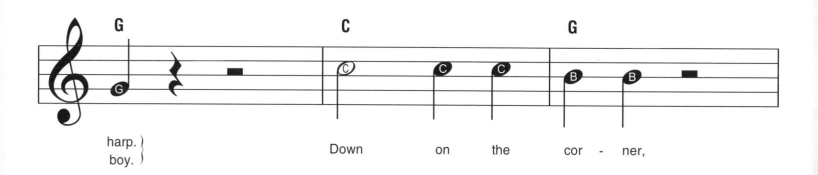

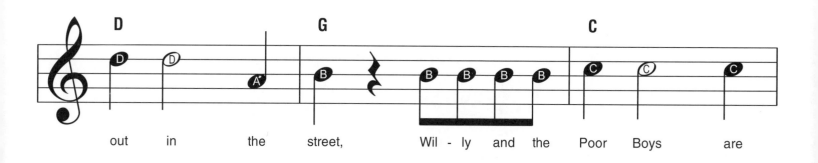

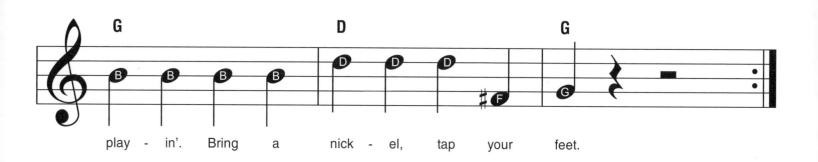

Dream On

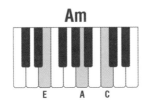

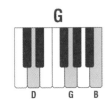
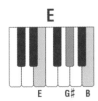
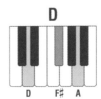

Words and Music by
Steven Tyler

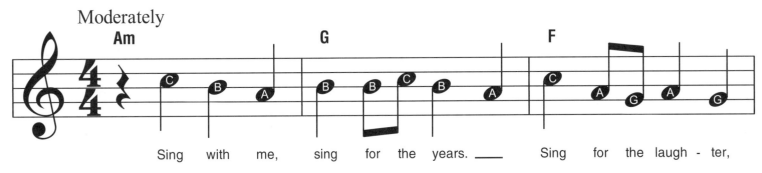

Sing with me, sing for the years. ____ Sing for the laugh-ter,

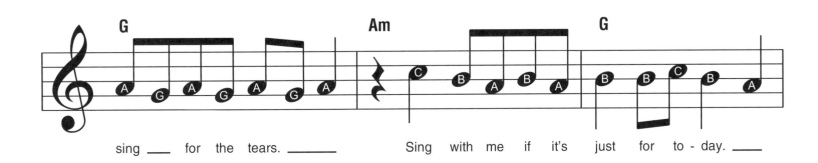

sing ____ for the tears. ____ Sing with me if it's just for to-day. ____

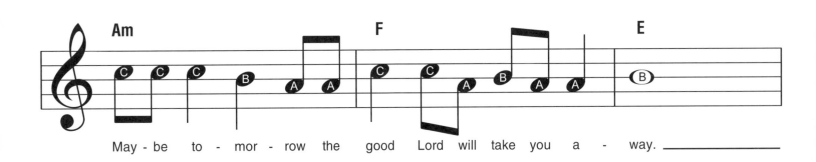

May-be to-mor-row the good Lord will take you a - way. ____

41

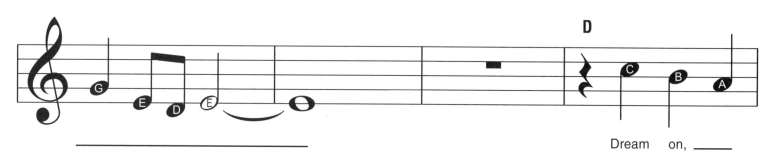

Dream on, _____

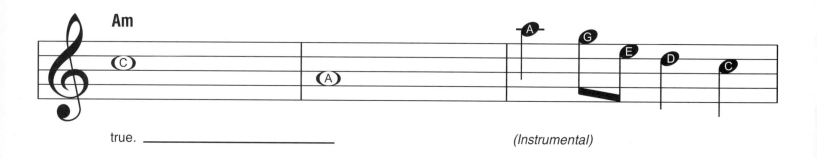

dream on, _____   dream on, _____   dream your - self a dream come

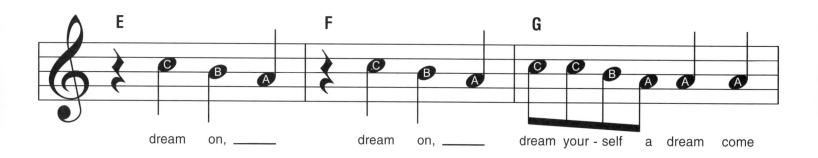

true. _____   *(Instrumental)*

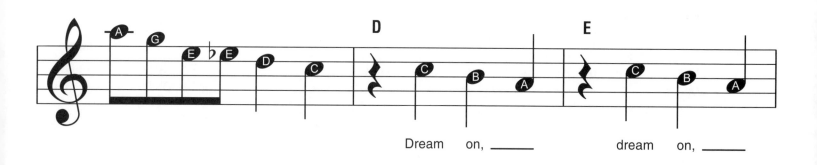

Dream on, _____   dream on, _____

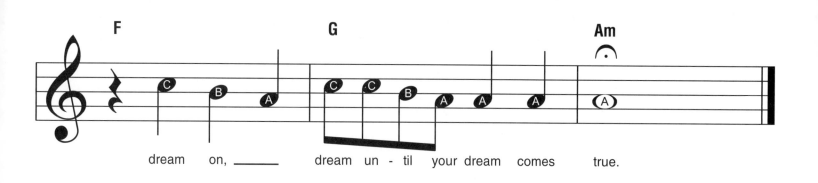

dream on, _____   dream un - til your dream comes true.

Dust in the Wind

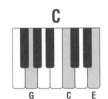
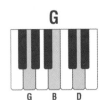

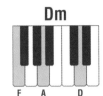
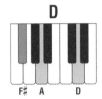

Words and Music by
Kerry Livgren

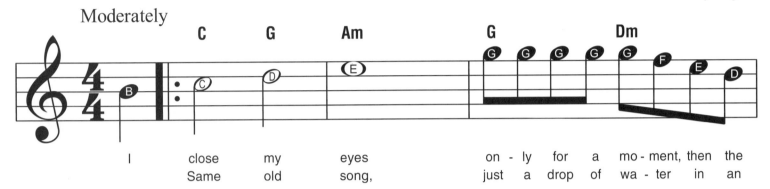

I close my eyes on-ly for a mo-ment, then the
Same old song, just a drop of wa-ter in an

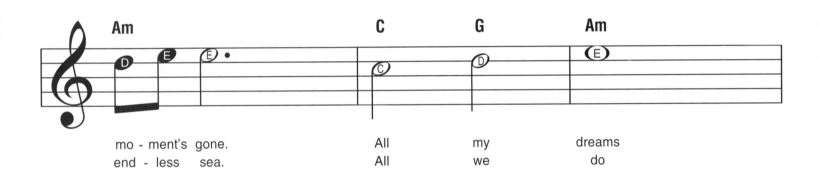

mo-ment's gone. All my dreams
end-less sea. All we do

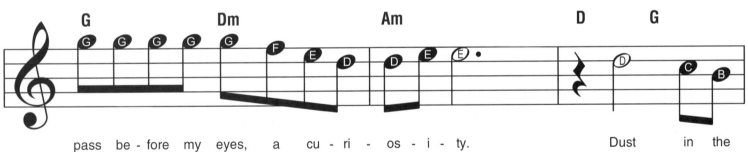

pass be-fore my eyes, a cu-ri-os-i-ty. Dust in the
crum-bles to the ground, though we re-fuse to see. Dust in the

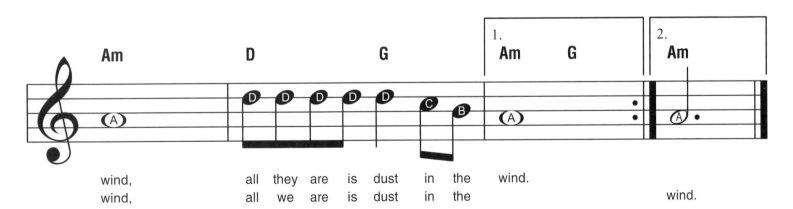

wind, all they are is dust in the wind.
wind, all we are is dust in the wind.

Fortunate Son

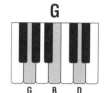 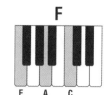 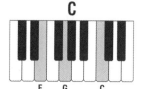

Words and Music by
John Fogerty

Fly Like an Eagle

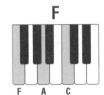
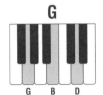
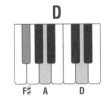

Words and Music by
Steve Miller

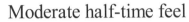

Moderate half-time feel

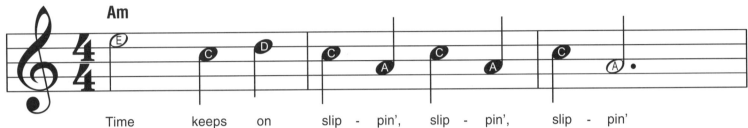

Time keeps on slip - pin', slip - pin', slip - pin'

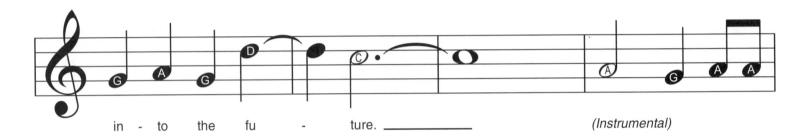

in - to the fu - ture. _____ (Instrumental)

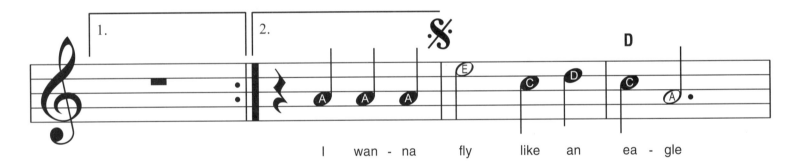

I wan - na fly like an ea - gle

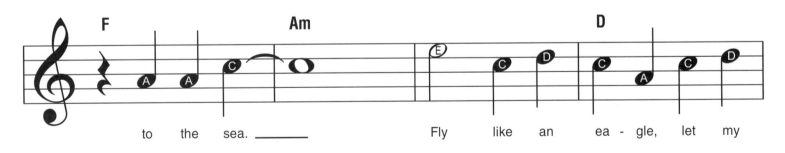

to the sea. _____ Fly like an ea - gle, let my

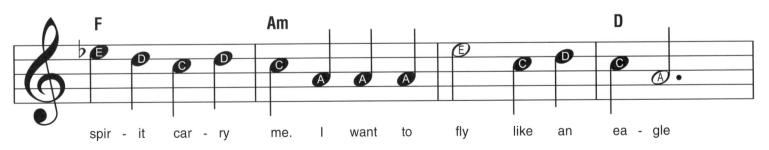

spir - it car - ry me. I want to fly like an ea - gle

Free Bird

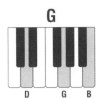
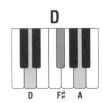
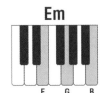
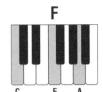
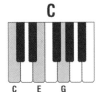

Words and Music by Allen Collins
and Ronnie Van Zant

Moderately slow

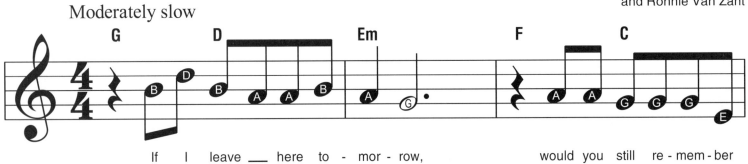

If I leave ___ here to - mor - row, would you still re - mem - ber

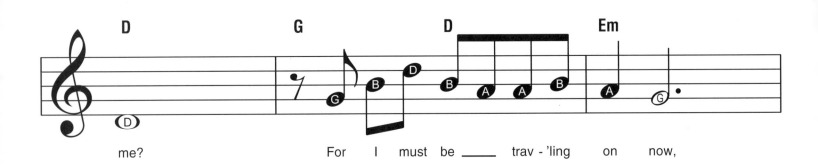

me? For I must be ___ trav - 'ling on now,

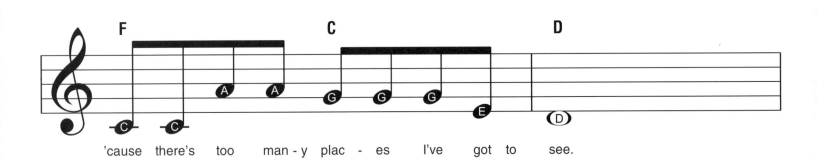

'cause there's too man - y plac - es I've got to see.

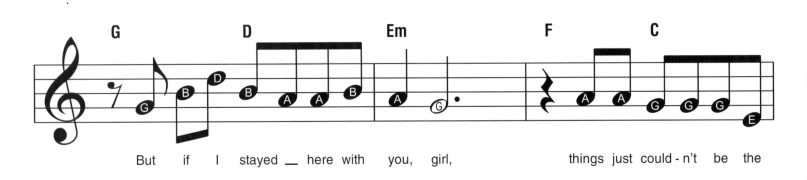

But if I stayed ___ here with you, girl, things just could - n't be the

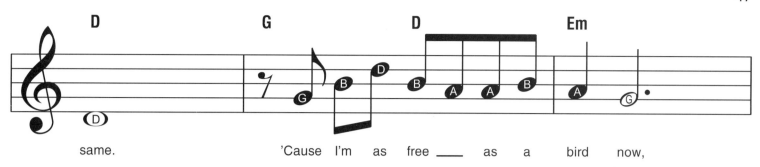

same.   'Cause I'm as free ____ as a bird now,

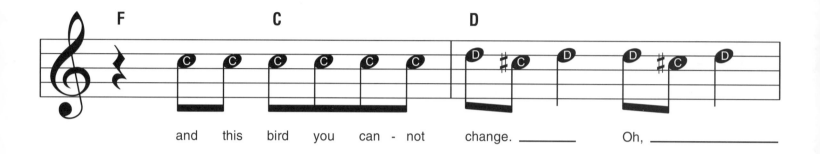

and this bird you can-not change. _____ Oh, _____

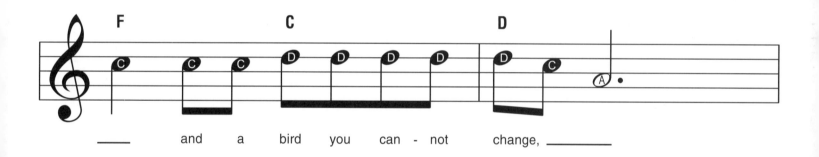

____ and a bird you can-not change, _____

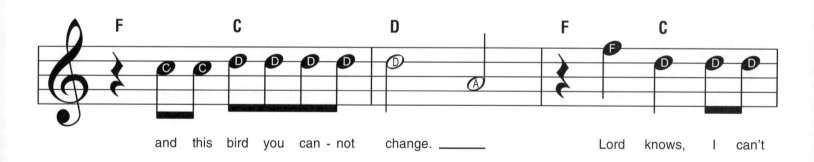

and this bird you can-not change. _____ Lord knows, I can't

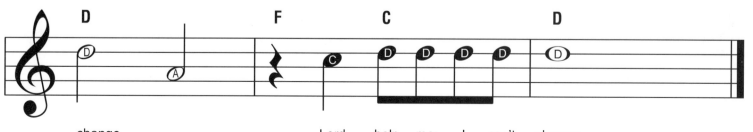

change. _____ Lord, help me; I can't change.

Free Fallin'

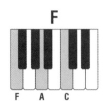
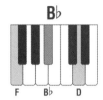
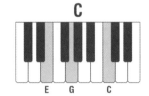

Words and Music by Tom Petty
and Jeff Lynne

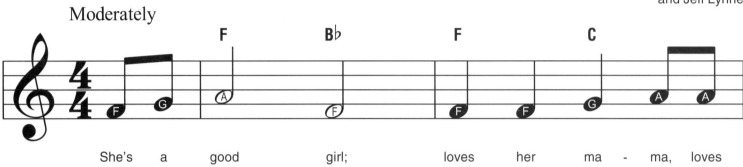

She's a good girl; loves her ma - ma, loves

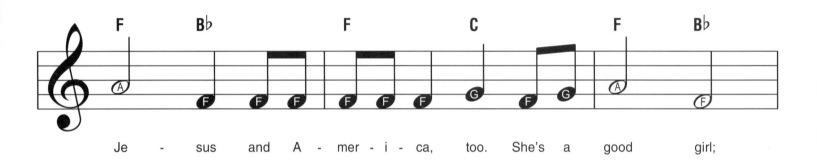

Je - sus and A - mer - i - ca, too. She's a good girl;

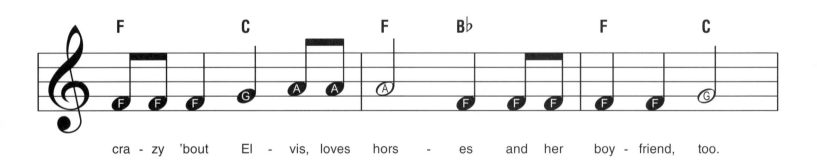

cra - zy 'bout El - vis, loves hors - es and her boy - friend, too.

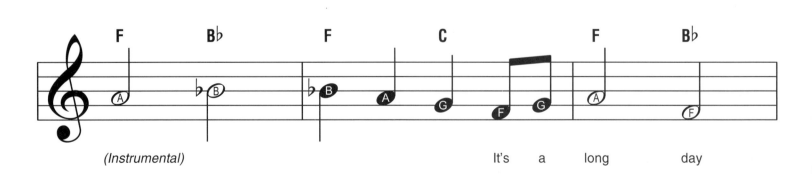

(Instrumental)   It's a long day

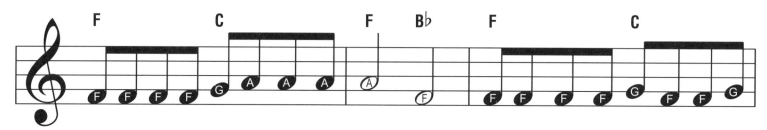

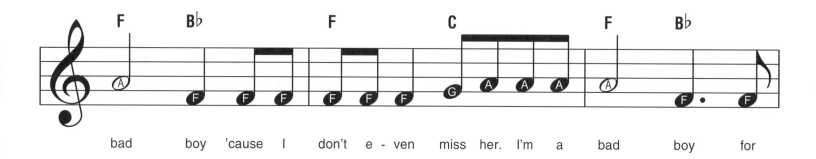

liv - in' in Re - se - da. There's a free - way run - nin' through the yard. And I'm a

bad boy 'cause I don't e - ven miss her. I'm a bad boy for

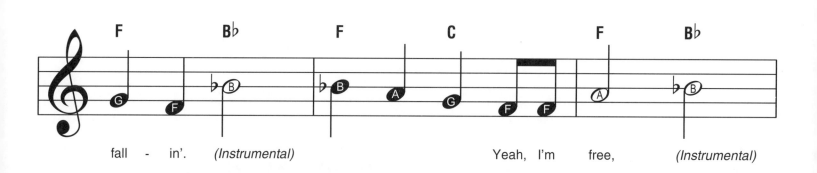

break - in' her heart. And I'm free, *(Instrumental)* free

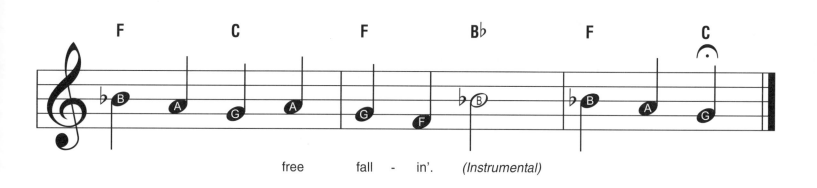

fall - in'. *(Instrumental)* Yeah, I'm free, *(Instrumental)*

free fall - in'. *(Instrumental)*

Get Back

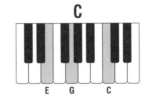

Words and Music by John Lennon
and Paul McCartney

Moderate Rock

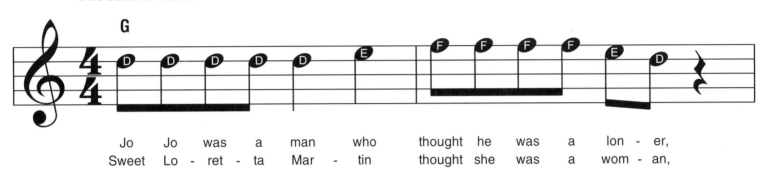

Jo Jo was a man who thought he was a lon - er,
Sweet Lo - ret - ta Mar - tin thought she was a wom - an,

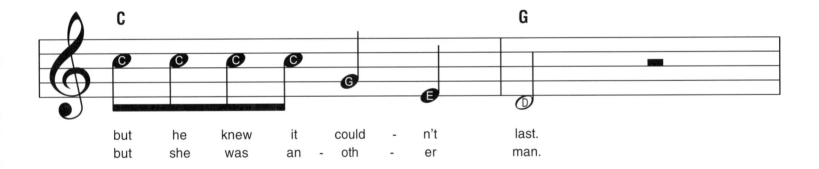

but he knew it could - n't last.
but she was an - oth - er man.

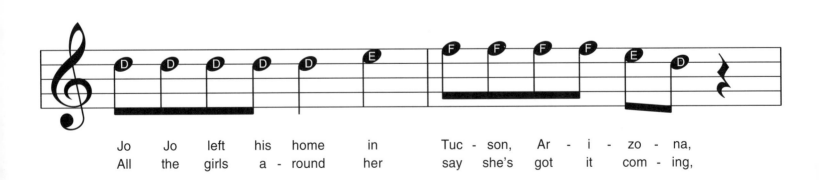

Jo Jo left his home in Tuc - son, Ar - i - zo - na,
All the girls a - round her say she's got it com - ing,

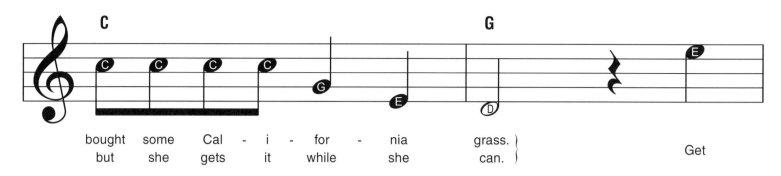

bought some Cal - i - for - nia grass.
but she gets it while she can.
Get

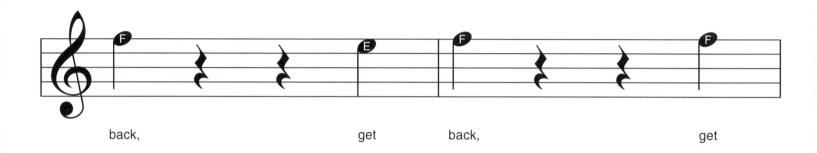

back, get back, get

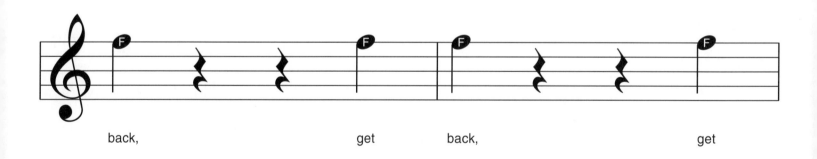

back to where you once be - longed. _____ Get

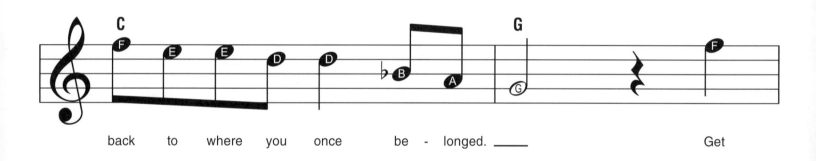

back, get back, get

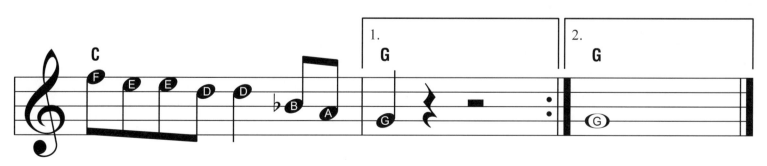

back to where you once be - longed. ___   ___

Go Your Own Way

 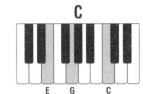 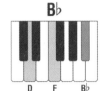

Words and Music by
Lindsey Buckingham

Moderately fast

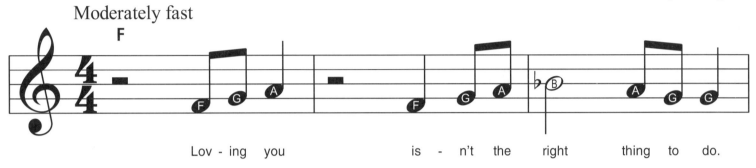

Lov - ing you   is - n't the   right   thing   to   do.

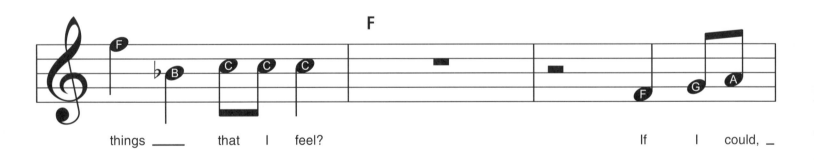

How   can   I _____   ev - er   change

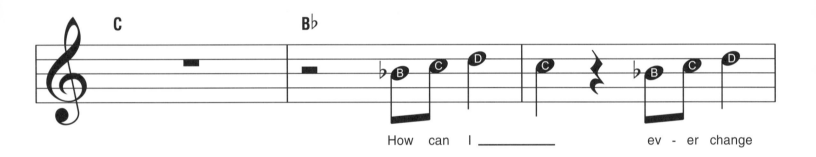

things ____ that   I   feel?   If   I   could, _

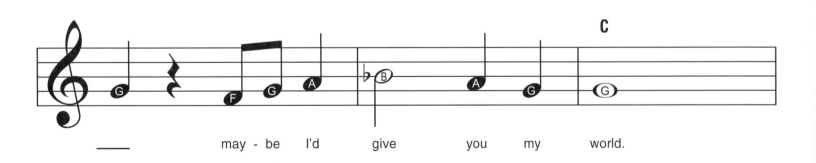

____   may - be   I'd   give   you   my   world.

53

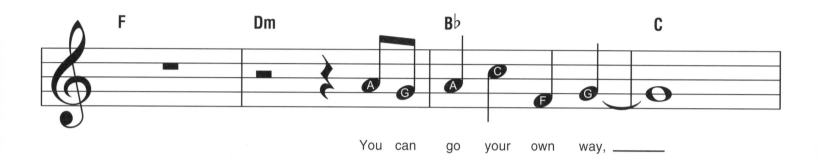

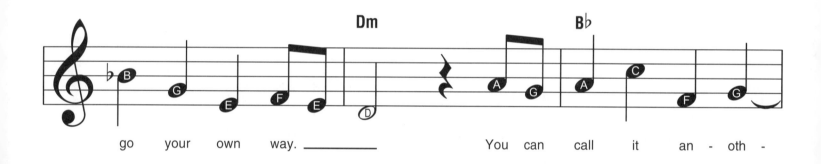

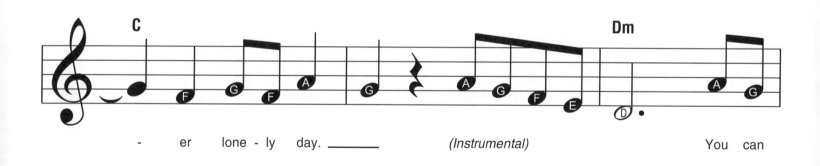

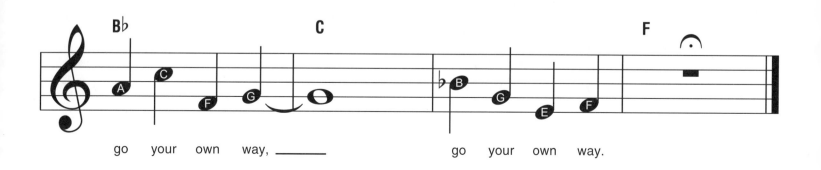

Hey Jude

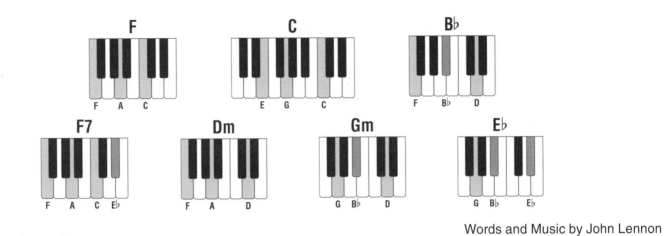

Words and Music by John Lennon
and Paul McCartney

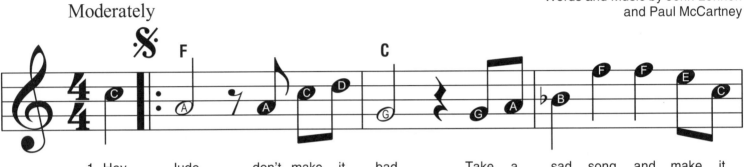

1. Hey Jude, don't make it bad. Take a sad song and make it
(2., 3.) *See additional lyrics*

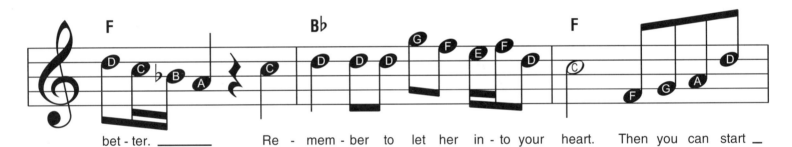

bet - ter. _____ Re - mem - ber to let her in - to your heart. Then you can start _

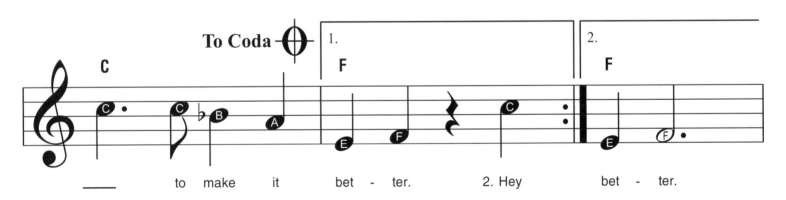

_ to make it bet - ter. 2. Hey bet - ter.

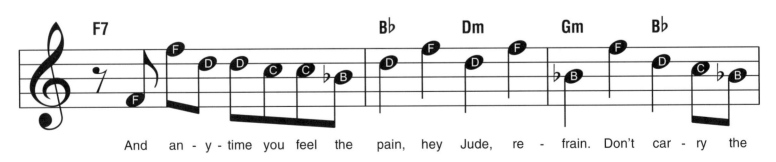

And an - y - time you feel the pain, hey Jude, re - frain. Don't car - ry the

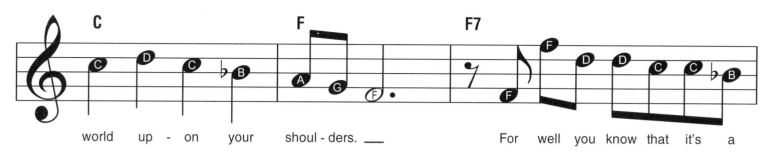

world up - on your shoul - ders. ___ For well you know that it's a

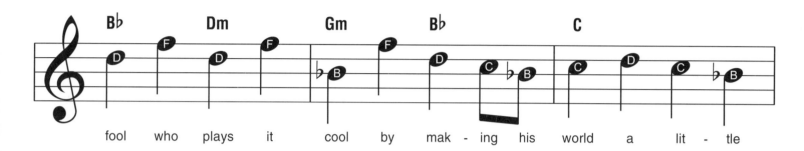

fool who plays it cool by mak - ing his world a lit - tle

D.S. al Coda
(Return to 𝄋, play to ⊕
and skip to Coda)

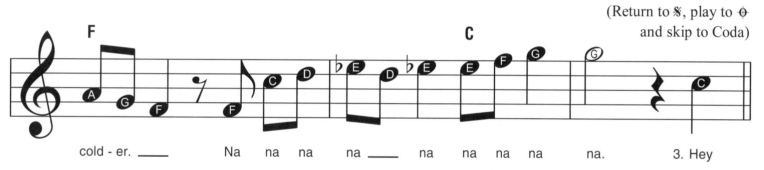

cold - er. ___ Na na na na ___ na na na na na. 3. Hey

CODA

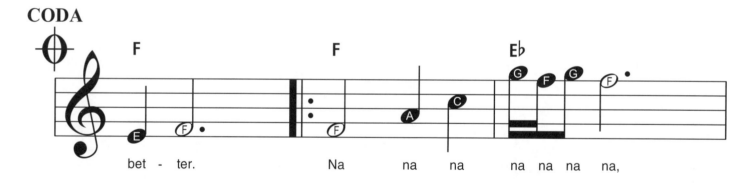

bet - ter. Na na na na na na na,

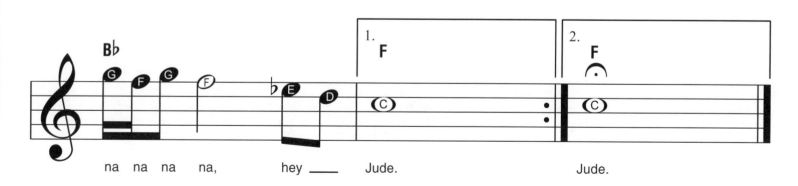

na na na na, hey ___ Jude. Jude.

Additional Lyrics

2. Hey Jude, don't be afraid.
You were made to go out and get her.
The minute you let her under your skin,
Then you begin to make it better.

3. Hey Jude, don't let me down.
You have found her, now go and get her.
Remember to let her into your heart,
Then you can start to make it better.

Hurts So Good

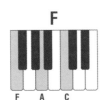
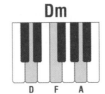
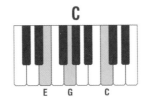

Words and Music by John Mellencamp
and George Green

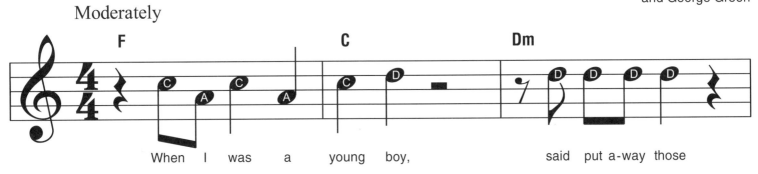

When I was a young boy, said put a-way those

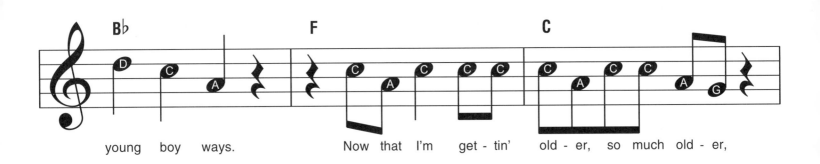

young boy ways. Now that I'm get - tin' old - er, so much old - er,

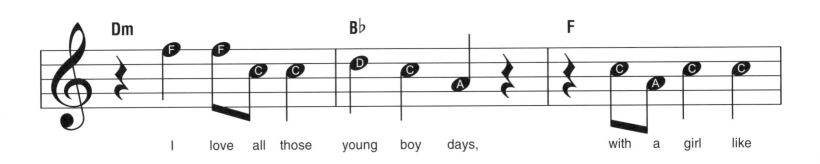

I love all those young boy days, with a girl like

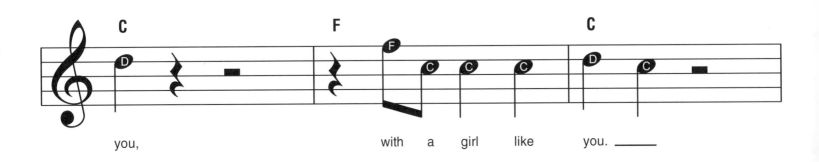

you, with a girl like you. _____

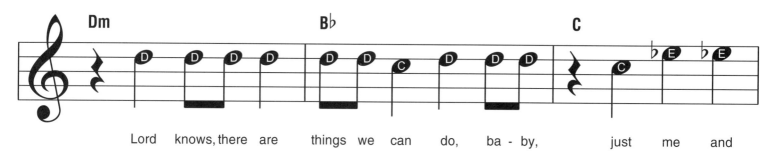

Lord knows, there are things we can do, ba - by, just me and

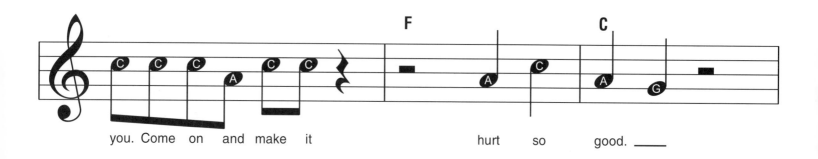

you. Come on and make it hurt so good. ____

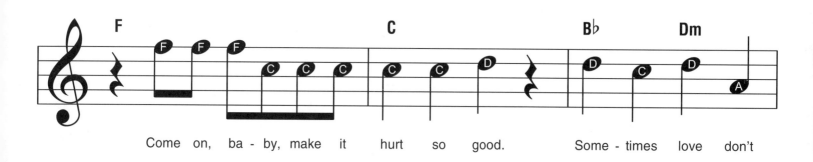

Come on, ba - by, make it hurt so good. Some - times love don't

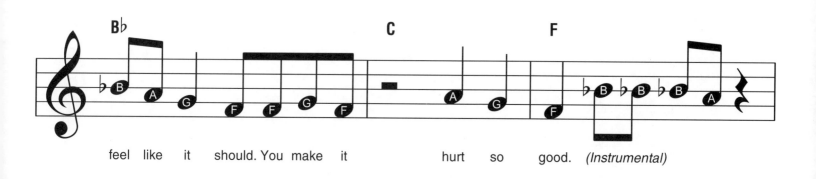

feel like it should. You make it hurt so good. *(Instrumental)*

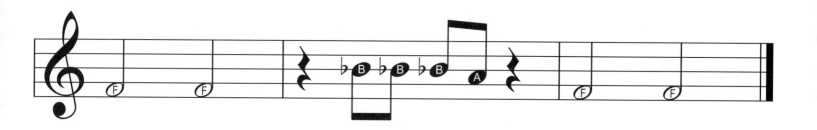

I Still Haven't Found What I'm Looking For

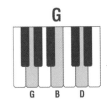
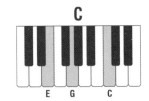
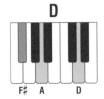

Words and Music by
U2

Moderate Rock

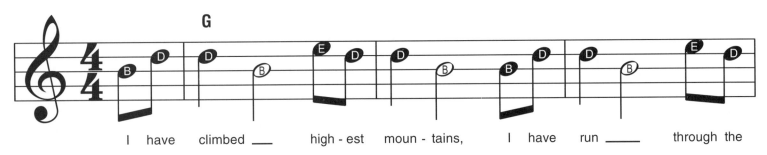

I have climbed ___ high-est moun-tains, I have run ___ through the

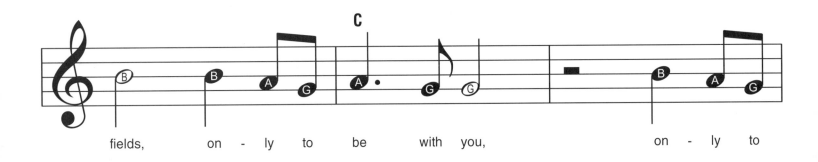

fields, on-ly to be with you, on-ly to

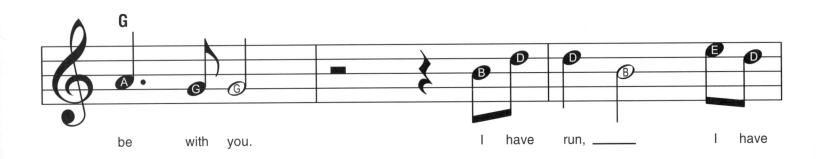

be with you. I have run, ___ I have

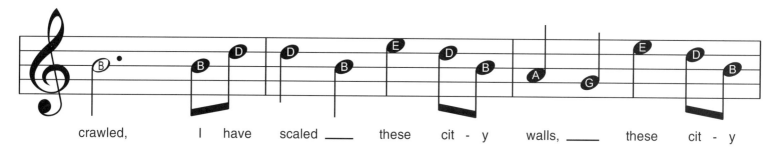

crawled, I have scaled ___ these cit - y walls, ___ these cit - y

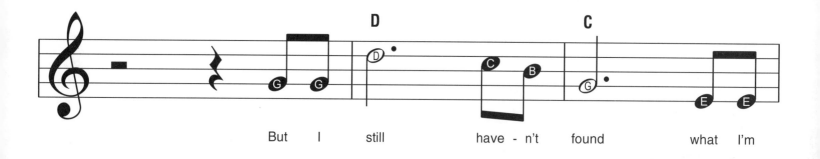

walls, ___ on - ly to be with you.

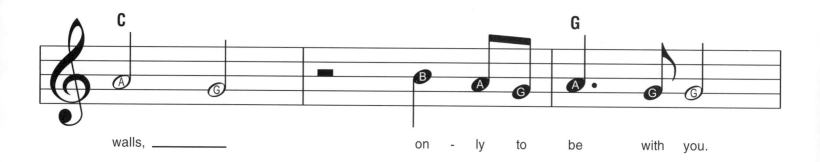

But I still have - n't found what I'm

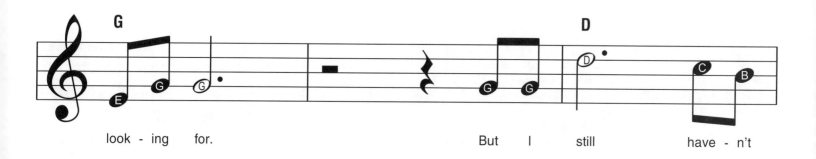

look - ing for. But I still have - n't

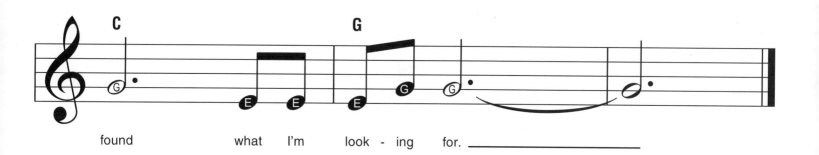

found what I'm look - ing for. ___

Jump

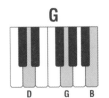 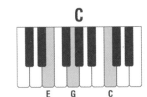 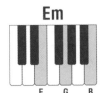 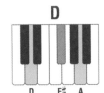 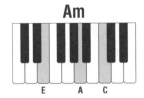

Words and Music by Edward Van Halen,
Alex Van Halen and David Lee Roth

61

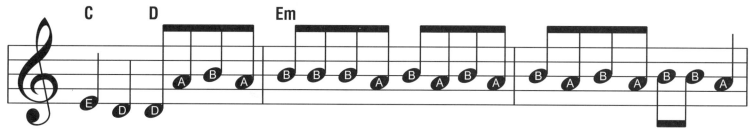

Ah, can't you see me stand-ing here? I got my back a-gainst the rec-ord ma-

chine. ____ I ain't the worst that you've seen. ____

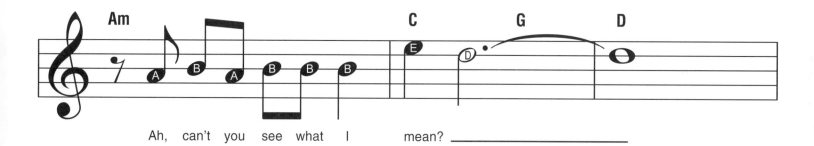

Ah, can't you see what I mean? _____

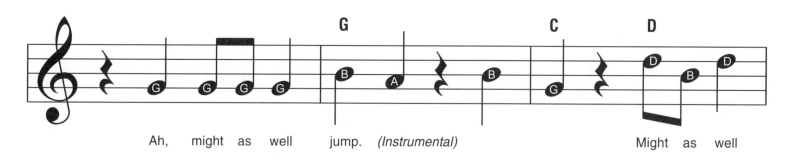

Ah, might as well jump. *(Instrumental)* Might as well

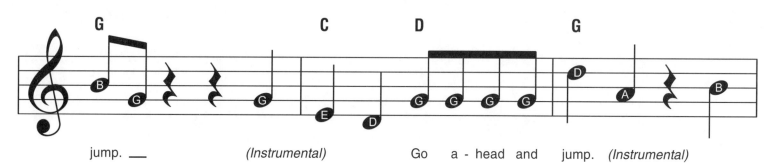

jump. __ *(Instrumental)* Go a-head and jump. *(Instrumental)*

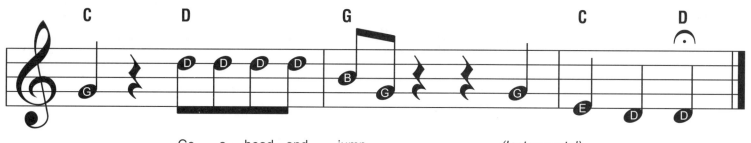

Go a-head and jump. __ *(Instrumental)*

Lay Down Sally

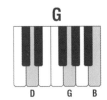
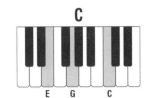
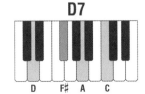

Words and Music by Eric Clapton,
Marcy Levy and George Terry

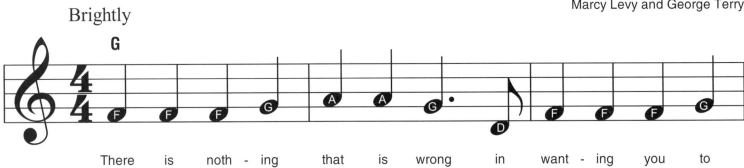

There is noth - ing that is wrong in want - ing you to

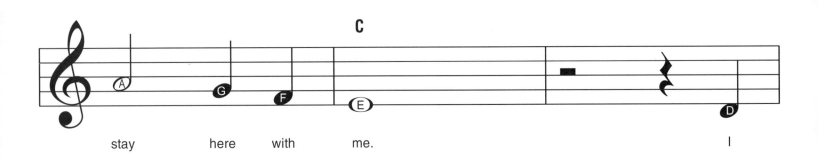

stay here with me. I

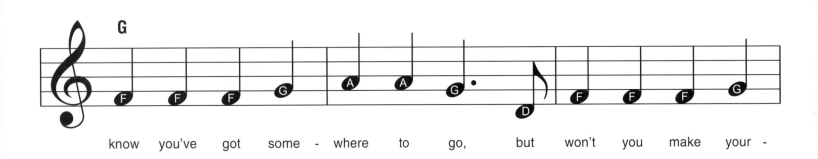

know you've got some - where to go, but won't you make your -

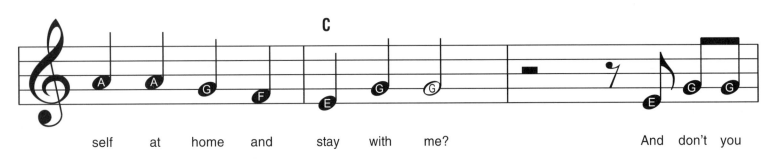

self at home and stay with me? And don't you

Livin' on a Prayer

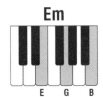
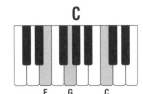
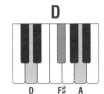
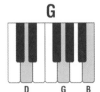

Words and Music by Jon Bon Jovi,
Desmond Child and Richie Sambora

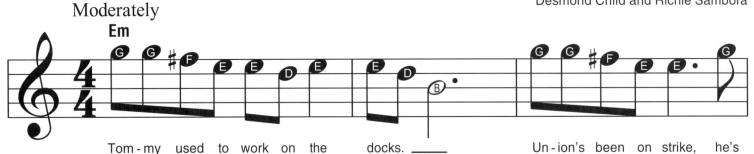

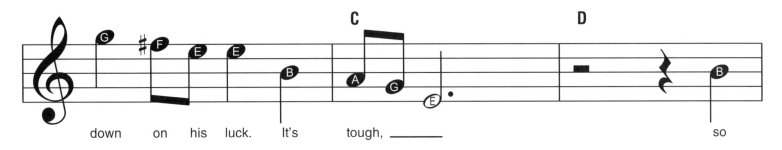

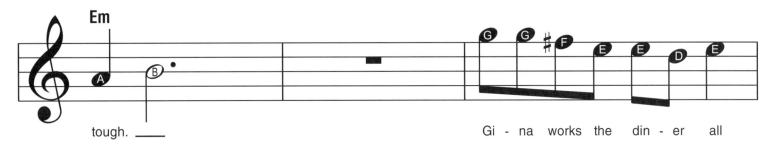

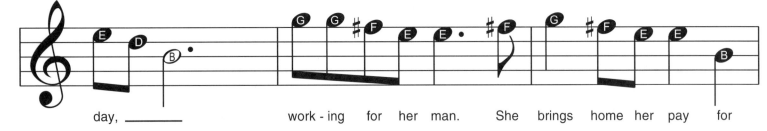

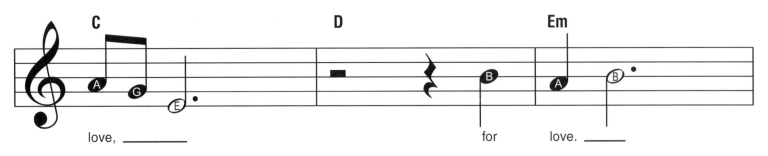

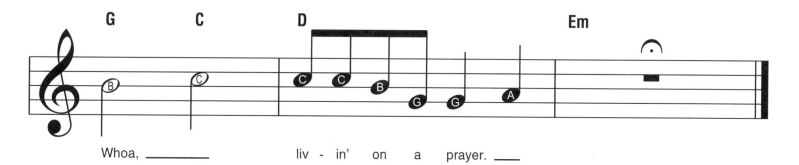

Maggie May

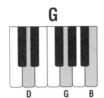
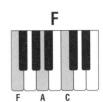
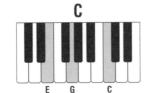

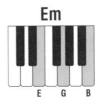

Words and Music by Rod Stewart
and Martin Quittenton

Moderately fast

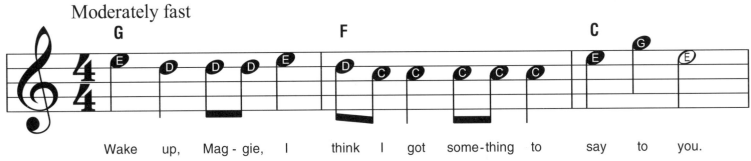

Wake up, Mag - gie, I think I got some-thing to say to you.

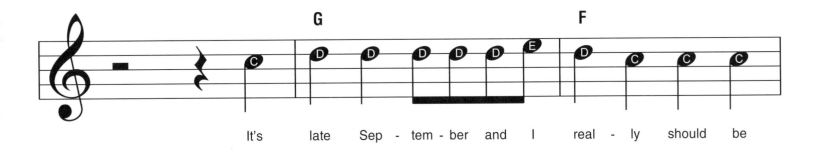

It's late Sep - tem - ber and I real - ly should be

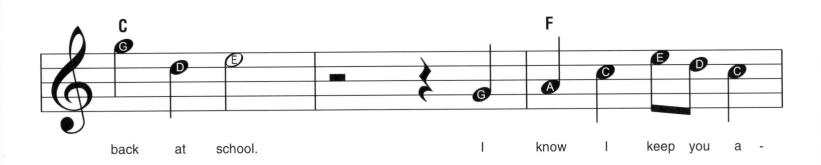

back at school. I know I keep you a -

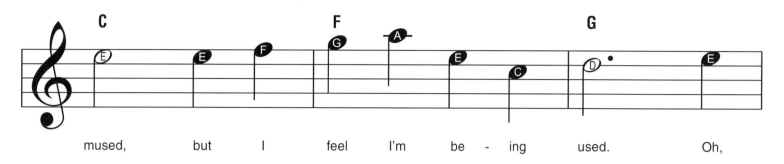

mused, but I feel I'm be - ing used. Oh,

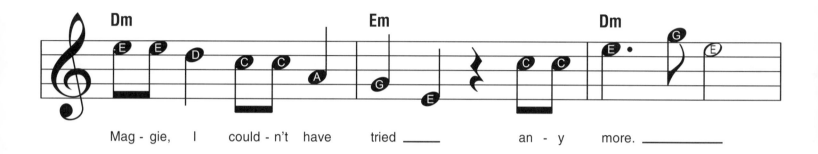

Mag - gie, I could - n't have tried _____ an - y more. _____

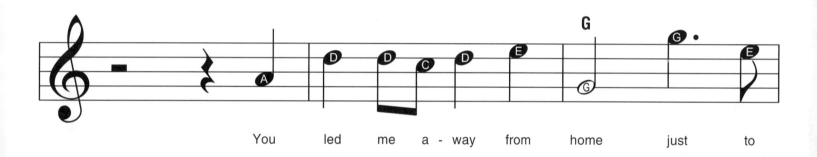

You led me a - way from home just to

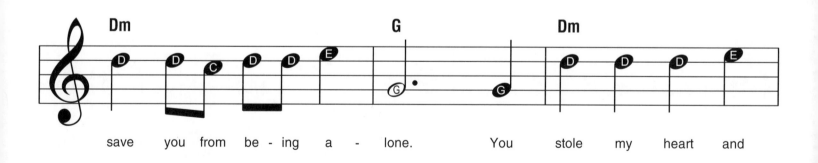

save you from be - ing a - lone. You stole my heart and

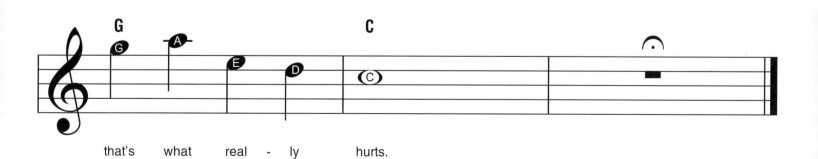

that's what real - ly hurts.

Me and Bobby McGee

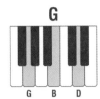
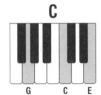

Words and Music by Kris Kristofferson
and Fred Foster

Moderately

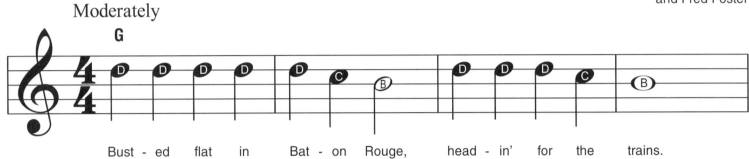

Bust - ed flat in Bat - on Rouge, head - in' for the trains.

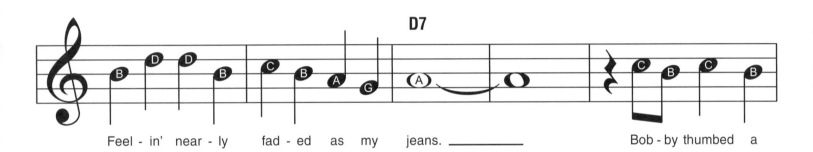

Feel - in' near - ly fad - ed as my jeans. _____ Bob - by thumbed a

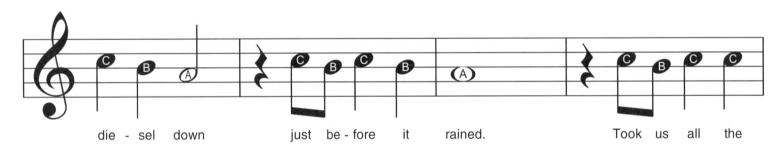

die - sel down just be - fore it rained. Took us all the

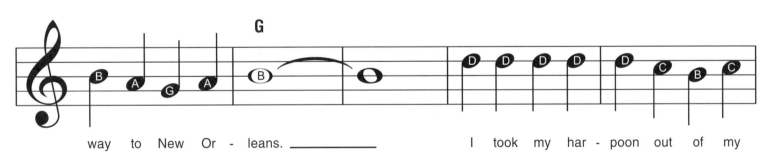

way to New Or - leans. _____ I took my har - poon out of my

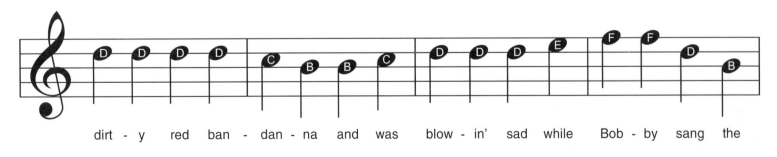

dirt - y red ban - dan - na and was blow - in' sad while Bob - by sang the

More Than a Feeling

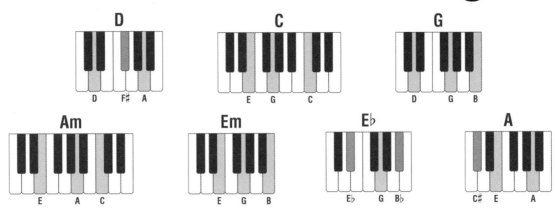

Words and Music by
Tom Scholz

Moderately

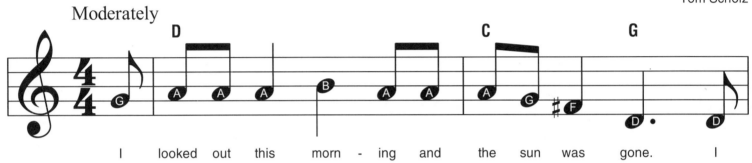

I looked out this morn-ing and the sun was gone. I

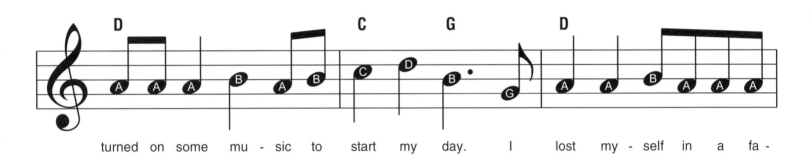

turned on some mu-sic to start my day. I lost my-self in a fa-

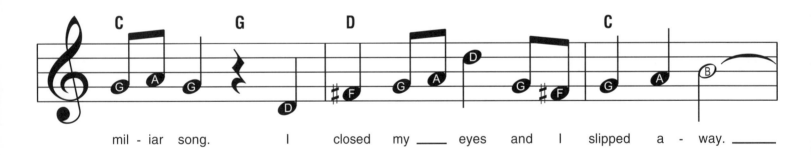

mil-iar song. I closed my ___ eyes and I slipped a-way. ___

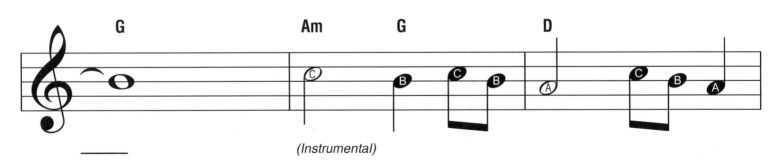

___ (Instrumental)

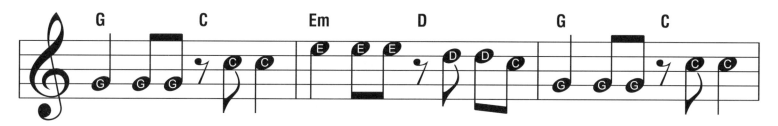

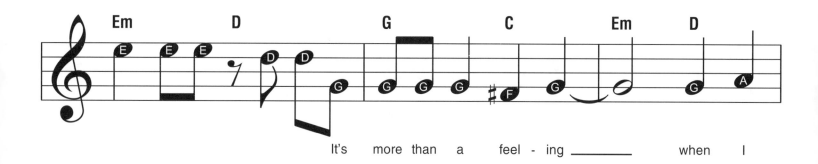

It's more than a feel - ing _____ when I

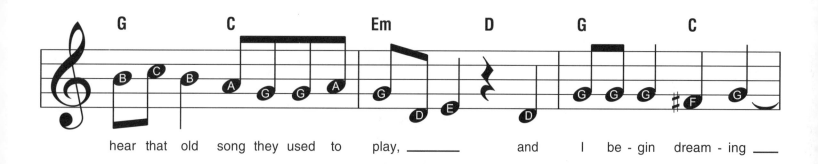

hear that old song they used to play, _____ and I be - gin dream - ing ___

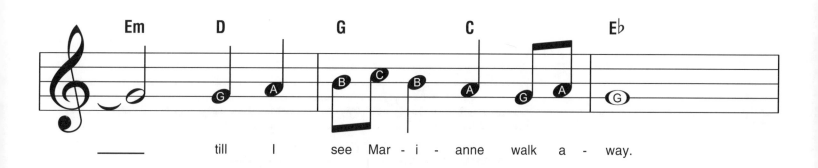

___ till I see Mar - i - anne walk a - way.

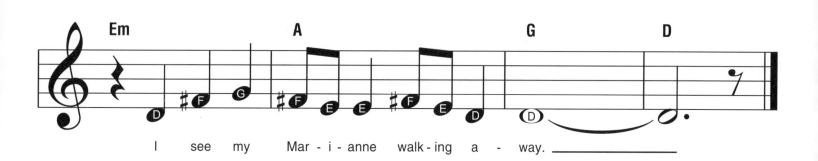

I see my Mar - i - anne walk - ing a - way. _____

Night Moves

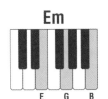
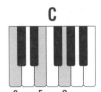
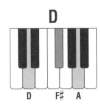
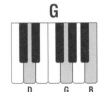

Words and Music by
Bob Seger

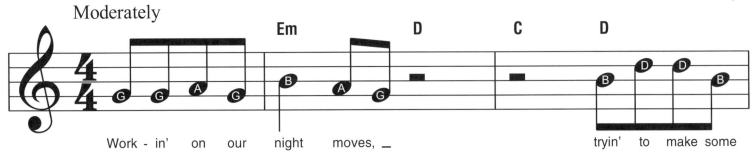

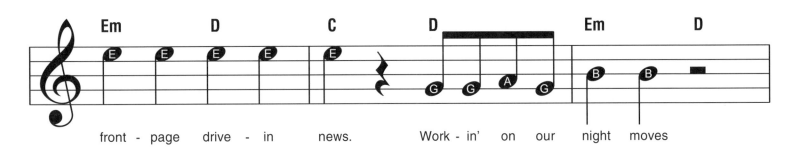

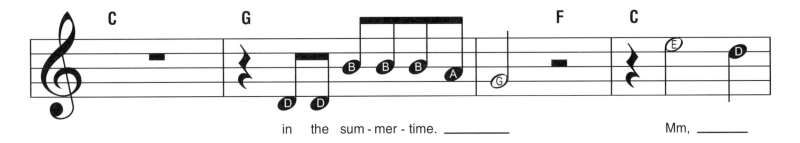

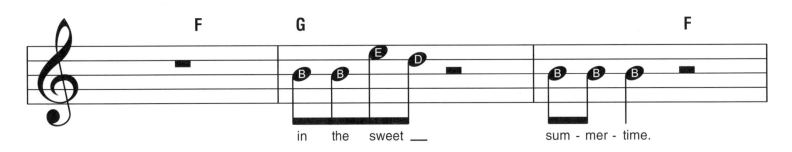

Somebody to Love

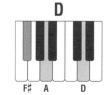
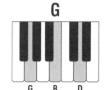
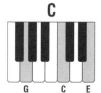

Words and Music by
Darby Slick

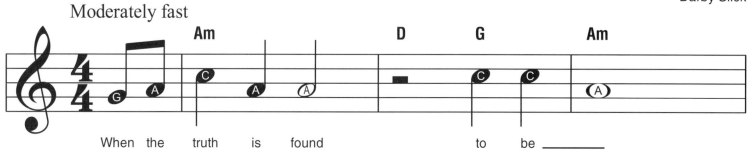

When the truth is found to be _____

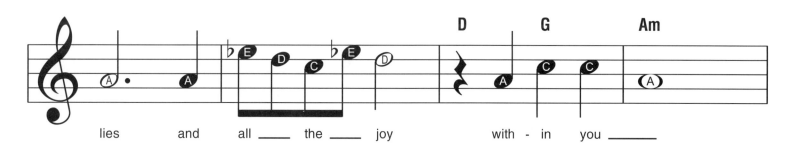

lies and all ____ the ____ joy with - in you _____

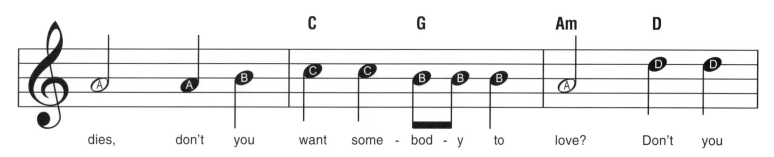

dies, don't you want some - bod - y to love? Don't you

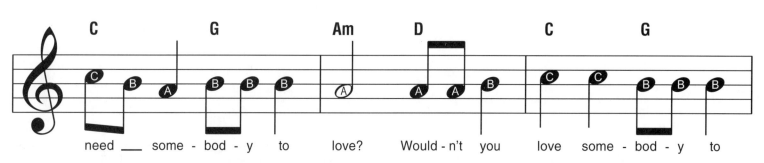

need ____ some - bod - y to love? Would - n't you love some - bod - y to

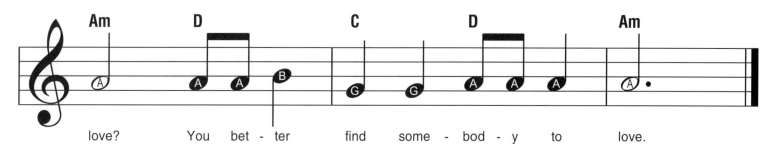

love? You bet - ter find some - bod - y to love.

Owner of a Lonely Heart

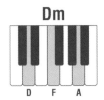
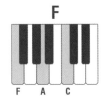
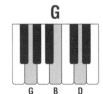
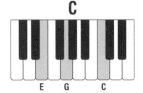

Words and Music by Trevor Rabin,
Jon Anderson, Chris Squire
and Trevor Horn

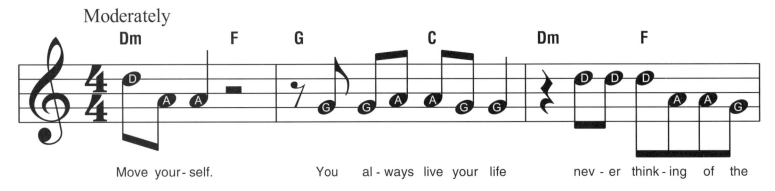

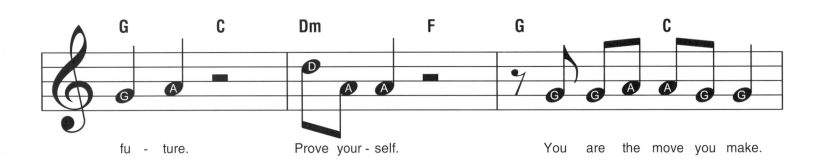

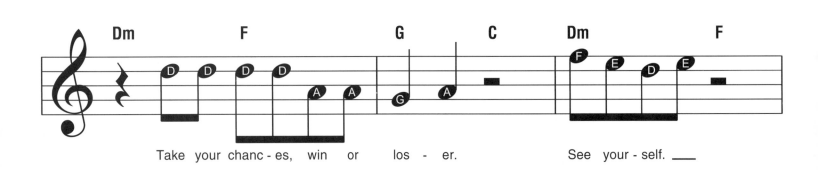

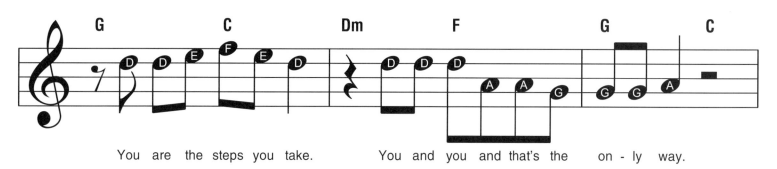

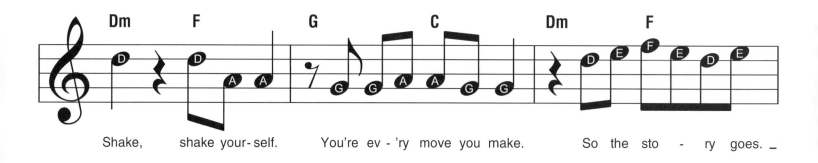

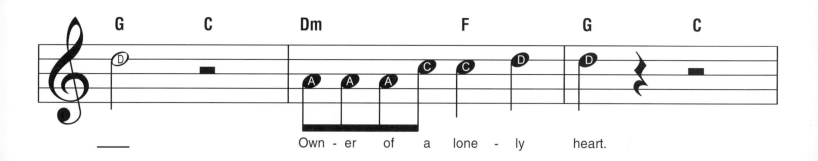

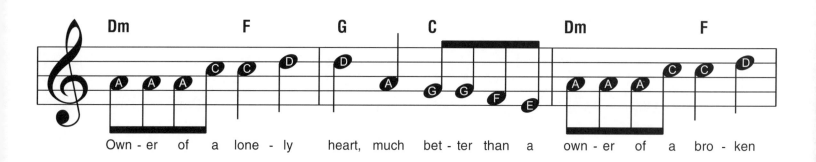

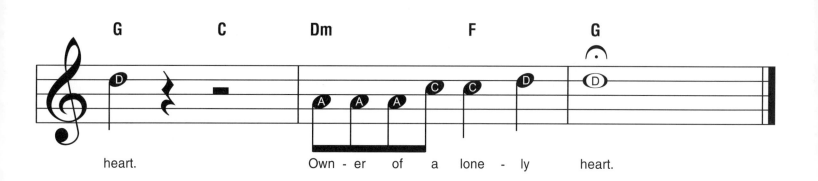

Peace of Mind

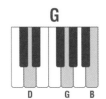
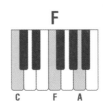
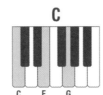
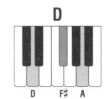

Words and Music by
Tom Scholz

Moderately fast

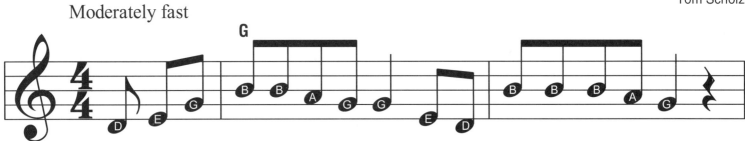

Now, if you're feel - in' kind - a low 'bout the dues you've been pay - in',

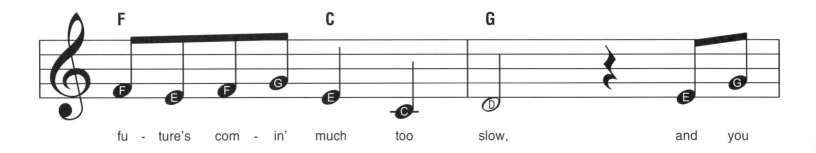

fu - ture's com - in' much too slow, and you

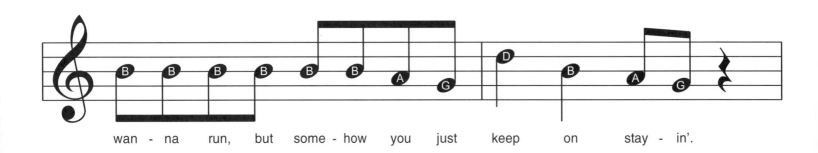

wan - na run, but some - how you just keep on stay - in'.

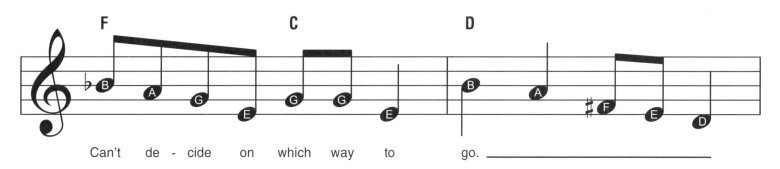

Can't de - cide on which way to go. _____

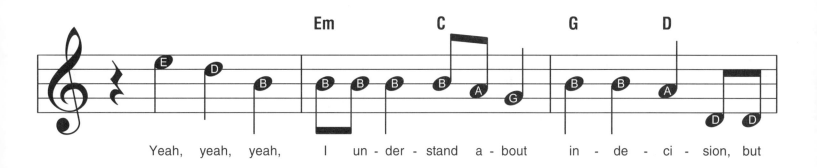

Yeah, yeah, yeah, I un - der - stand a - bout in - de - ci - sion, but

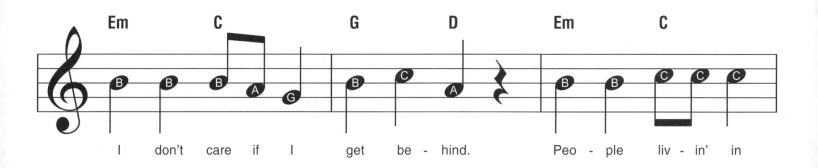

I don't care if I get be - hind. Peo - ple liv - in' in

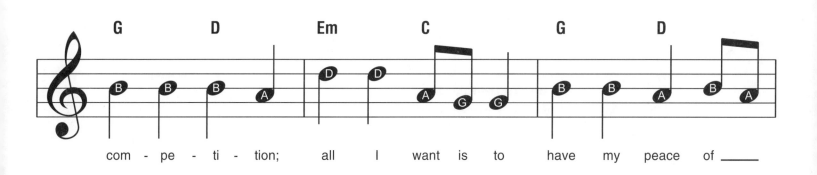

com - pe - ti - tion; all I want is to have my peace of _____

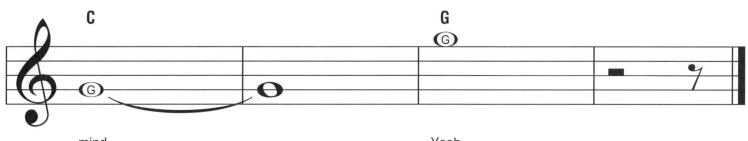

mind. _____ Yeah.

Pink Houses

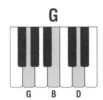
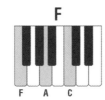
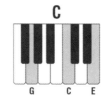
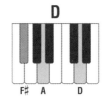

Words and Music by
John Mellencamp

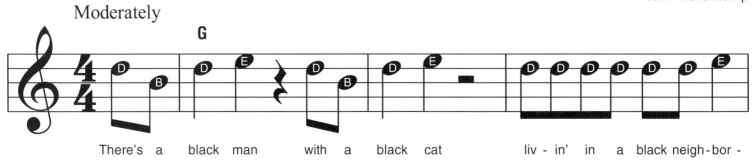

There's a black man with a black cat liv - in' in a black neigh - bor -

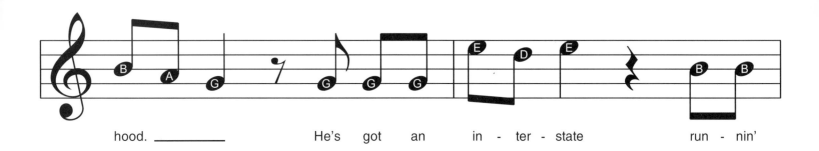

hood. _____ He's got an in - ter - state run - nin'

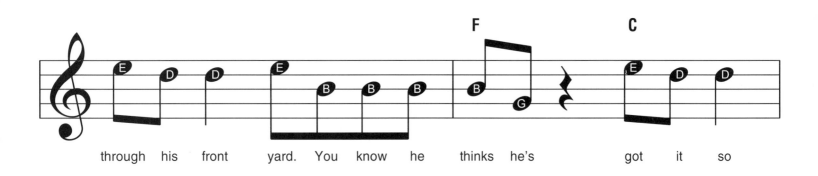

through his front yard. You know he thinks he's got it so

good. ____ And there's a wom - an in the

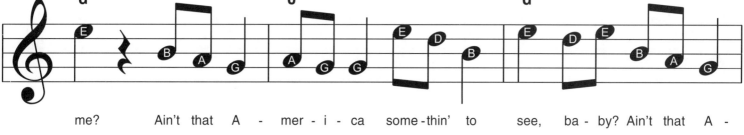

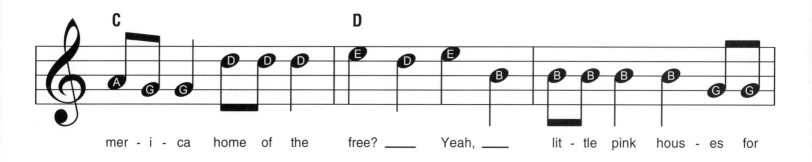

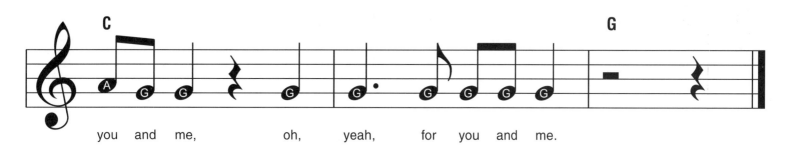

Ramblin' Man

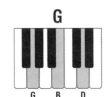
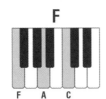
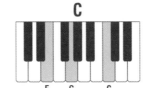
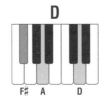

Words and Music by
Dickey Betts

Moderate half-time feel

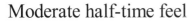

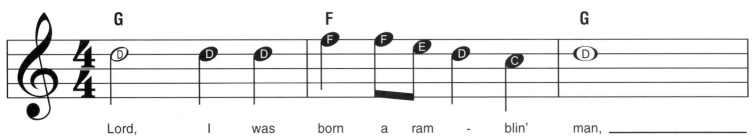

Lord, I was born a ram - blin' man, _____

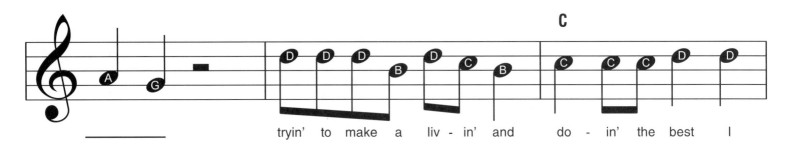

_____ tryin' to make a liv - in' and do - in' the best I

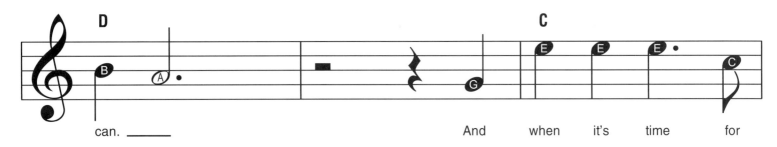

can. _____ And when it's time for

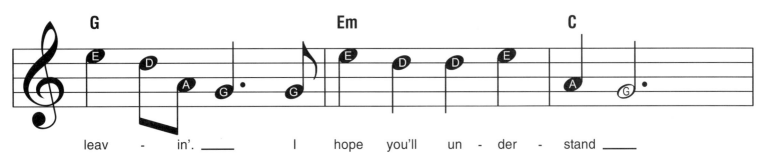

leav - in'. _____ I hope you'll un - der - stand _____

To Coda

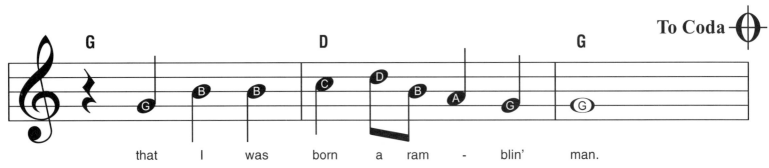

that I was born a ram - blin' man.

Well, my fa - ther was a gam - bler down in Geor - gia, _____ and he wound up on _____ the wrong end of a gun. _____ And I was born in the back _____ seat of a Grey - hound bus, _____ roll - in' down High - way For - ty -

D.C. al Coda
(Return to beginning,
play to ⊕ and skip to Coda)

CODA

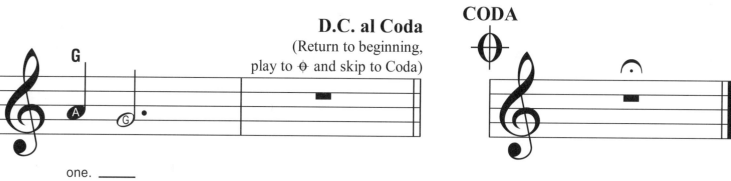

one. _____

Revolution

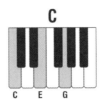
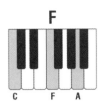
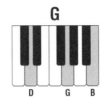
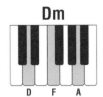

Words and Music by John Lennon
and Paul McCartney

Rock Shuffle

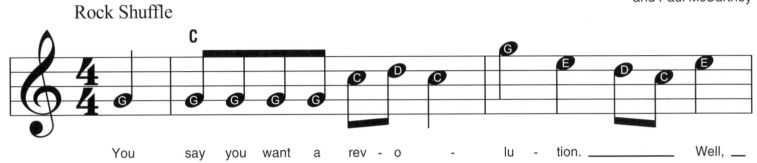

You say you want a rev - o - lu - tion. _____ Well, __

_____ you know _____ we all want to change the world.

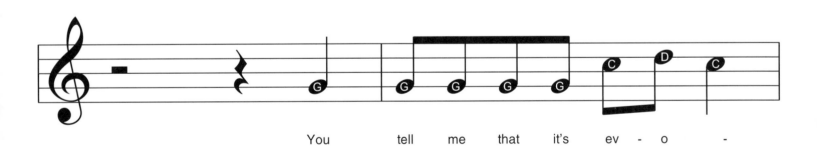

You tell me that it's ev - o -

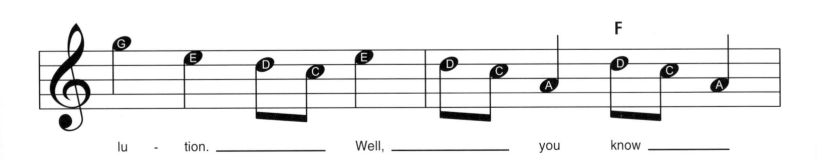

lu - tion. _____ Well, _____ you know _____

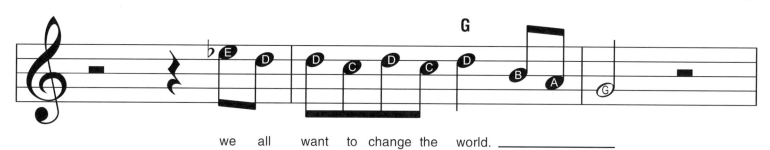

we all want to change the world. _____

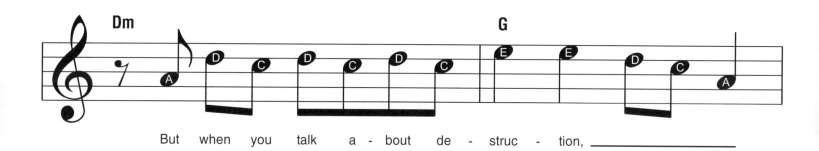

But when you talk a - bout de - struc - tion, _____

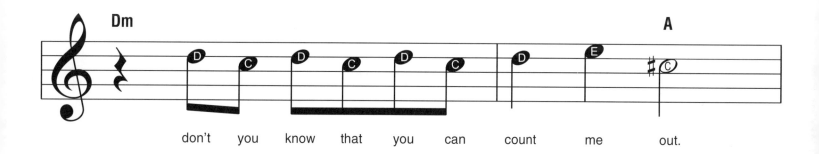

don't you know that you can count me out.

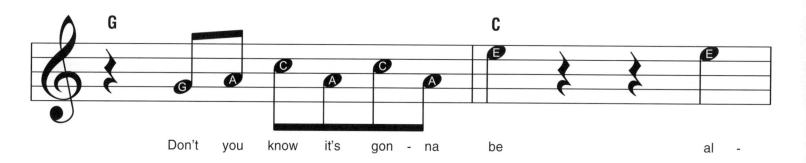

Don't you know it's gon - na be al -

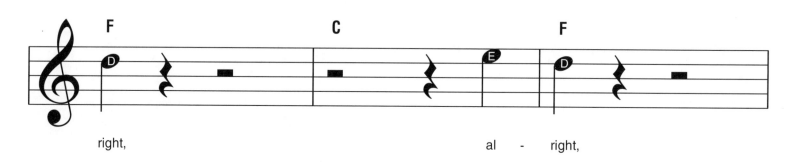

right, al - right,

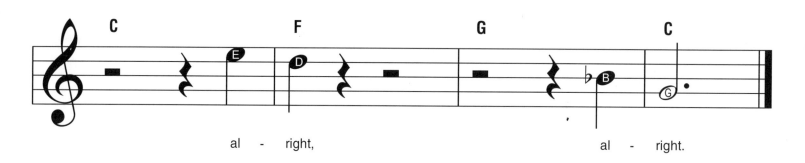

al - right, al - right.

Rhiannon

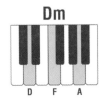
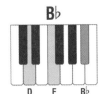

Words and Music by
Stevie Nicks

Moderately

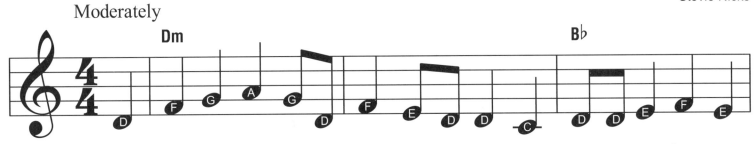

Rhi - an - non rings like a bell through the night. And would - n't you love to

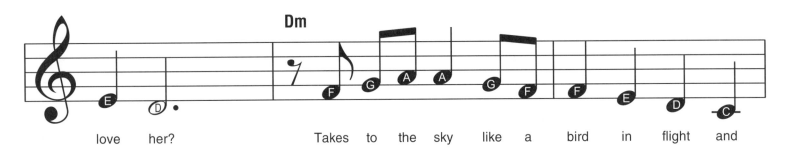

love her? Takes to the sky like a bird in flight and

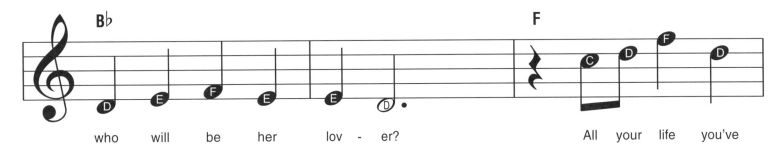

who will be her lov - er? All your life you've

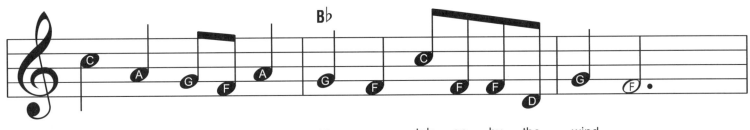

nev - er seen a wom - an ____ tak - en by the wind. ____

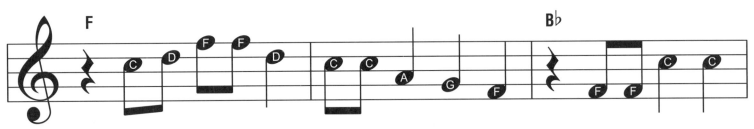

Would you stay if she prom - ised you heav - en? Will you ev - er

Rikki Don't Lose That Number

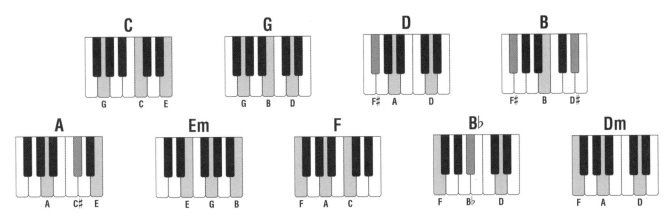

Words and Music by Walter Becker
and Donald Fagen

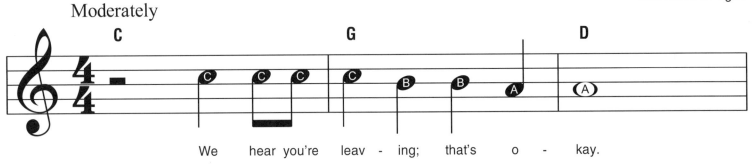

We hear you're leav - ing; that's o - kay.

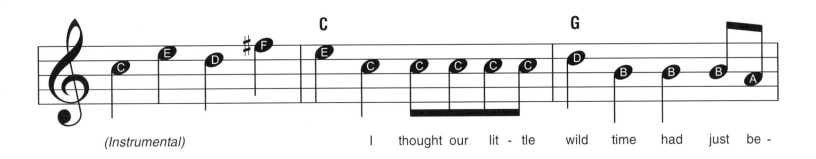

(Instrumental)   I thought our lit - tle wild time had just be -

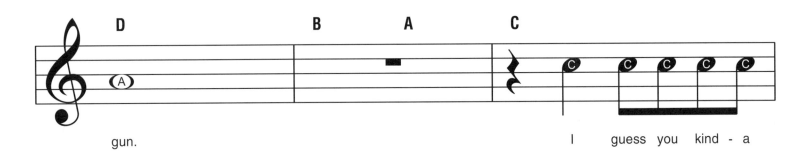

gun.   I guess you kind - a

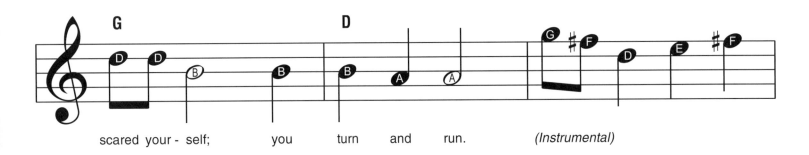

scared your - self; you turn and run.   (Instrumental)

Rosanna

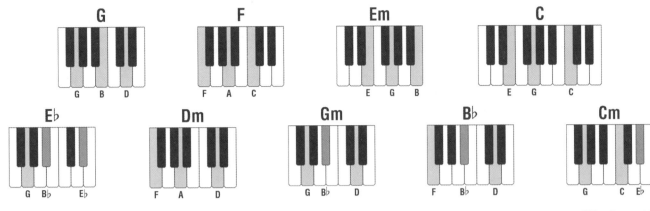

Words and Music by
David Paich

Bright Shuffle

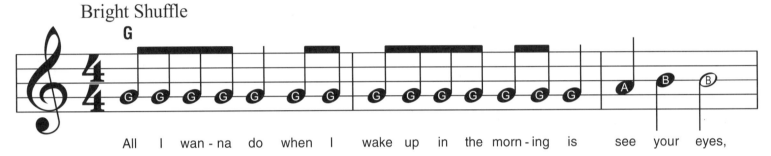

All I wan-na do when I wake up in the morn-ing is see your eyes,

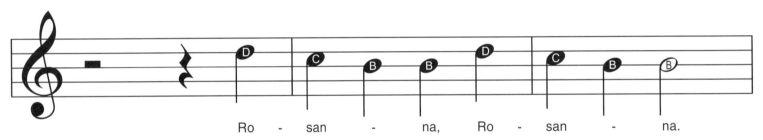

Ro - san - na, Ro - san - na.

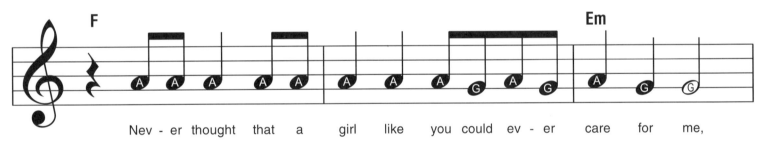

Nev - er thought that a girl like you could ev - er care for me,

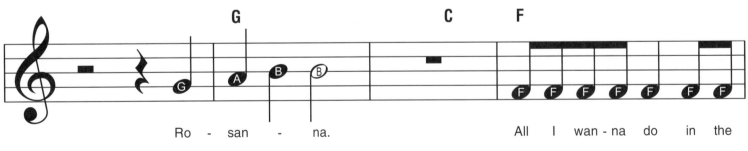

Ro - san - na. All I wan-na do in the

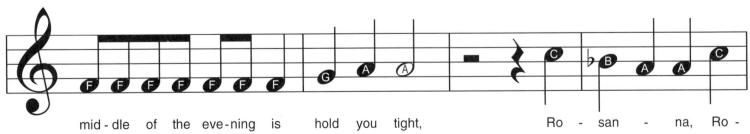

mid-dle of the eve-ning is hold you tight, Ro - san - na, Ro -

Runnin' Down a Dream

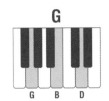
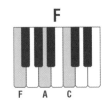
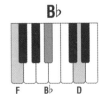

Words and Music by Tom Petty,
Jeff Lynne and Mike Campbell

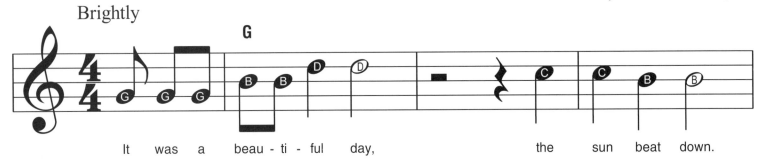

It was a beau-ti-ful day, the sun beat down.

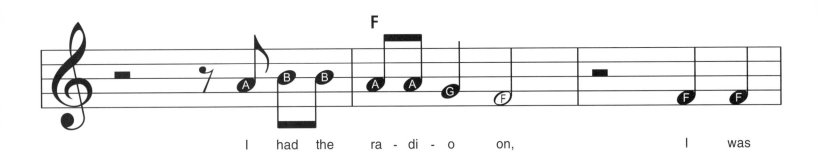

I had the ra-di-o on, I was

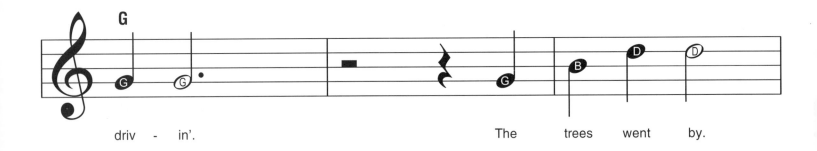

driv - in'. The trees went by.

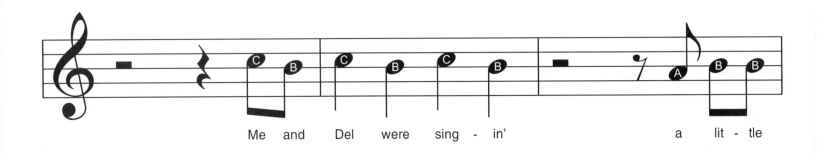

Me and Del were sing-in' a lit-tle

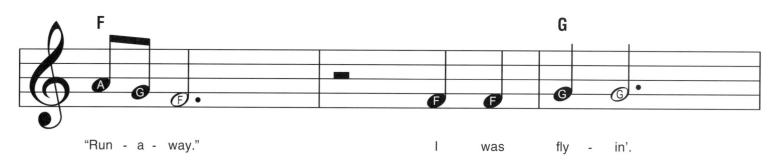

"Run - a - way." I was fly - in'.

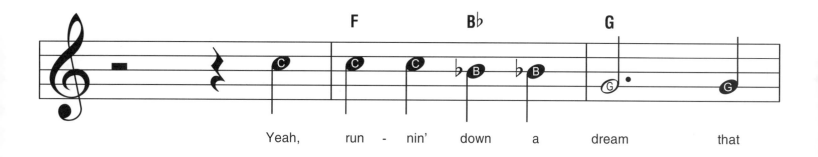

Yeah, run - nin' down a dream that

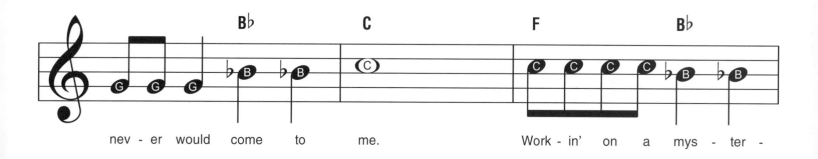

nev - er would come to me. Work - in' on a mys - ter -

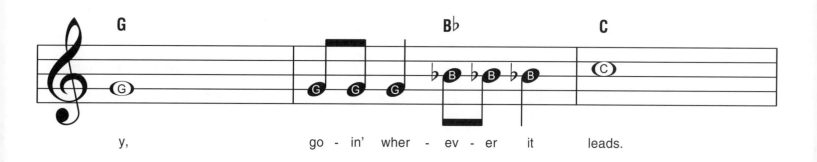

y, go - in' wher - ev - er it leads.

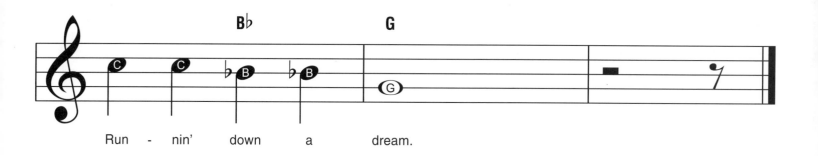

Run - nin' down a dream.

Smoke on the Water

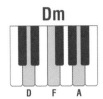
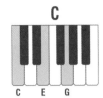
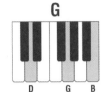
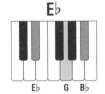

Words and Music by Ritchie Blackmore,
Ian Gillan, Roger Glover,
Jon Lord and Ian Paice

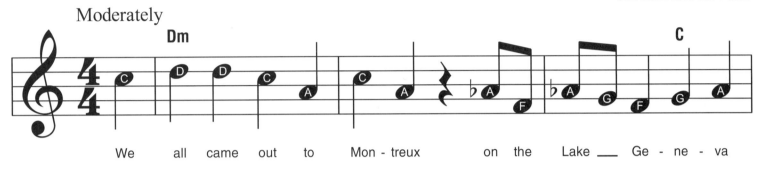

We all came out to Mon - treux on the Lake ___ Ge - ne - va

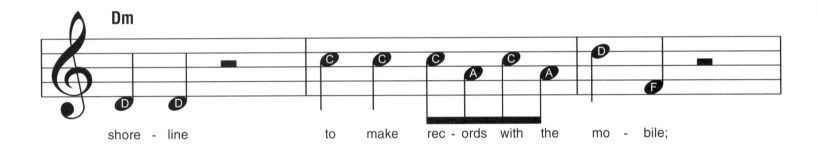

shore - line to make rec - ords with the mo - bile;

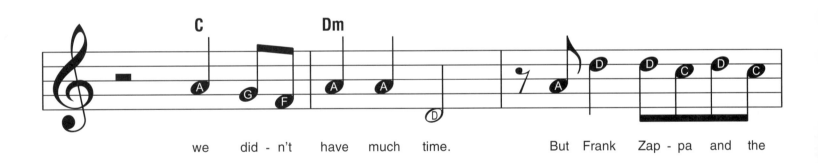

we did - n't have much time. But Frank Zap - pa and the

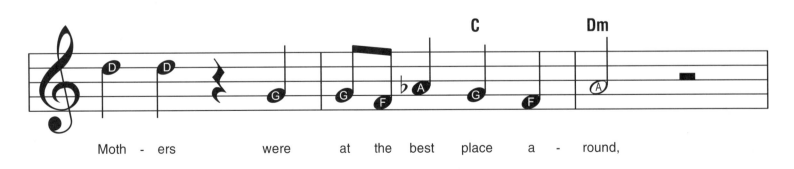

Moth - ers were at the best place a - round,

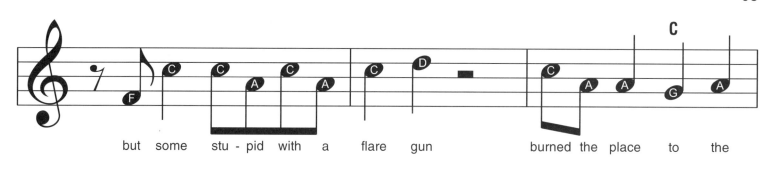

but some stu-pid with a flare gun burned the place to the

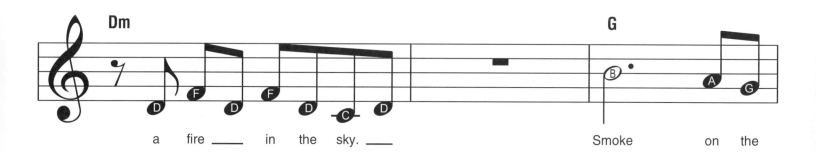

ground. Smoke on the wa - ter,

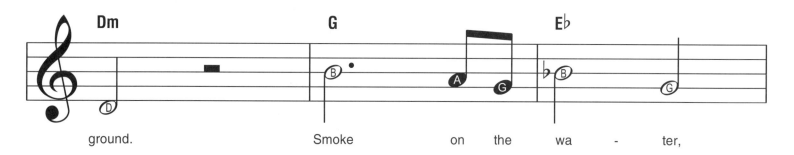

a fire ___ in the sky. ___ Smoke on the

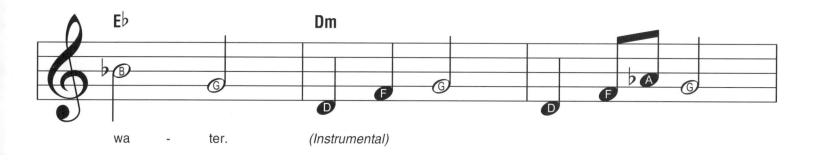

wa - ter. *(Instrumental)*

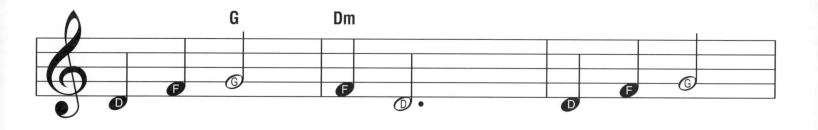

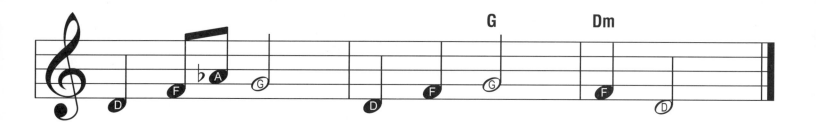

93

Start Me Up

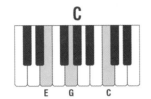
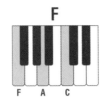

Words and Music by Mick Jagger
and Keith Richards

If you start me up, if you start me up, I'll nev-er stop. ___

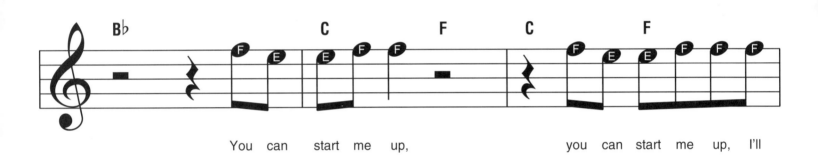

You can start me up, you can start me up, I'll

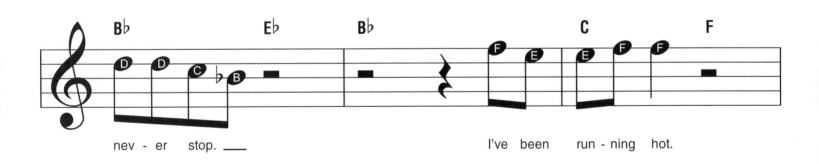

nev-er stop. ___ I've been run-ning hot.

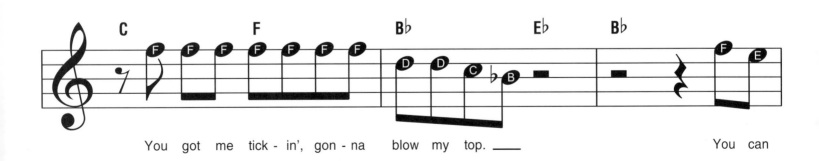

You got me tick-in', gon-na blow my top. ___ You can

start me up. You can start me up, I nev - er stop, nev - er stop,

nev - er stop, nev - er stop. ___ You make a grown man cry. _____

You make a grown man cry. _____ You make a grown man

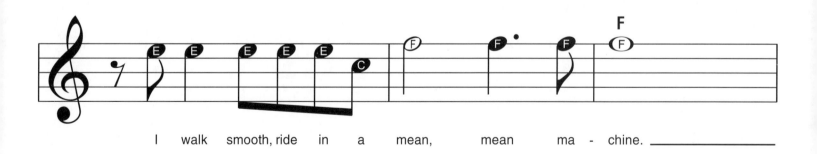

cry. _____ Spread out the oil, the gas - o - line.

I walk smooth, ride in a mean, mean ma - chine. _____

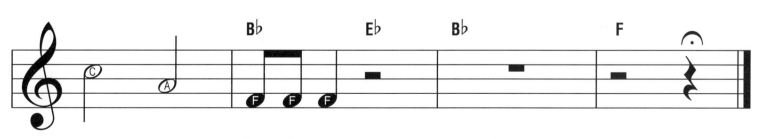

_____ Start it up.

Surrender

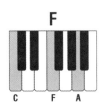
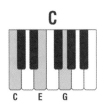
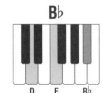
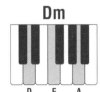

Words and Music by
Rick Nielsen

Moderately fast

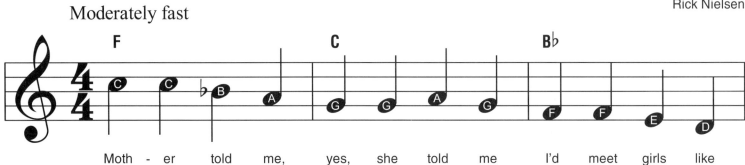

Moth - er told me, yes, she told me I'd meet girls like

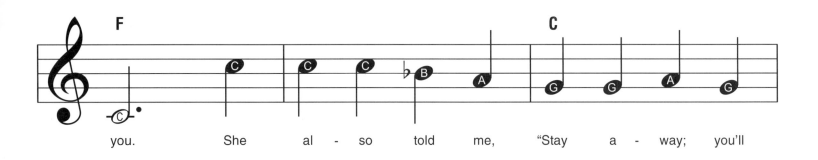

you. She al - so told me, "Stay a - way; you'll

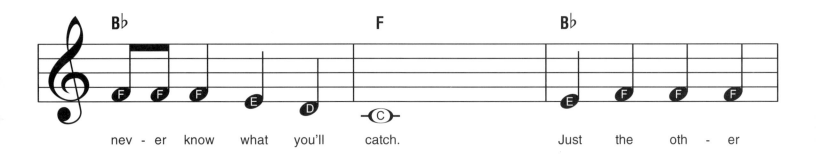

nev - er know what you'll catch. Just the oth - er

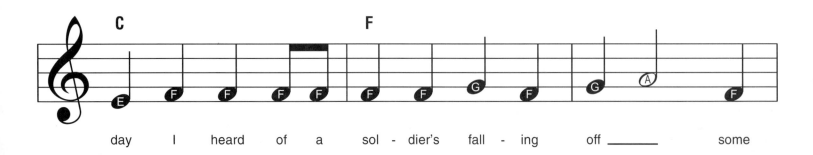

day I heard of a sol - dier's fall - ing off _____ some

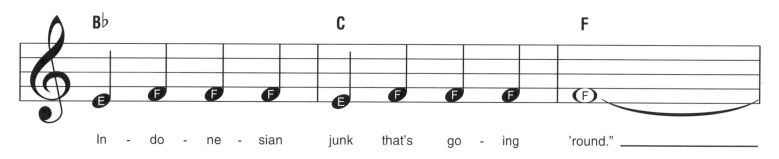

In - do - ne - sian junk that's go - ing 'round." _____

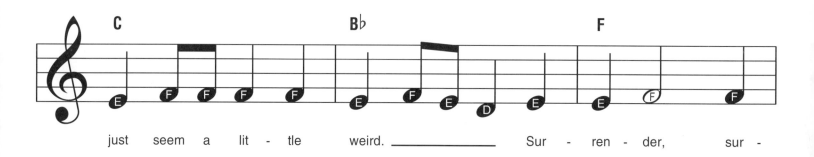

_____ Mom - my's all right, Dad - dy's all right, they

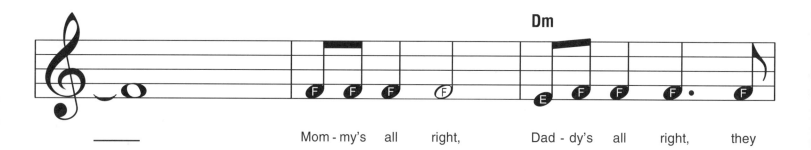

just seem a lit - tle weird. _____ Sur - ren - der, sur -

ren - der, but don't give your - self a - way, _____

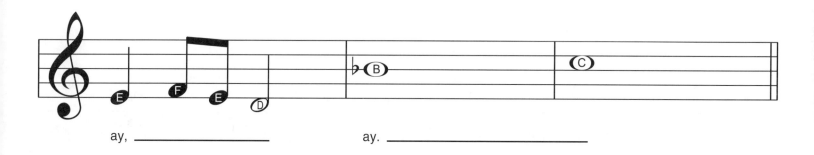

ay, _____ ay. _____

(Instrumental)

Sweet Home Alabama

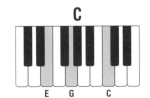 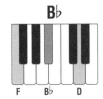 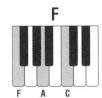

Words and Music by Ronnie Van Zant,
Ed King and Gary Rossington

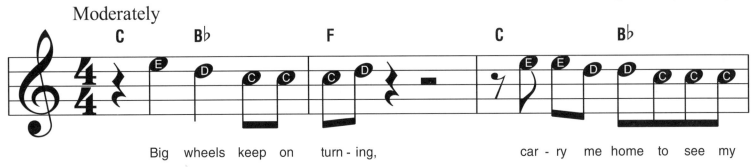

Big wheels keep on turn - ing,   car - ry me home to see my

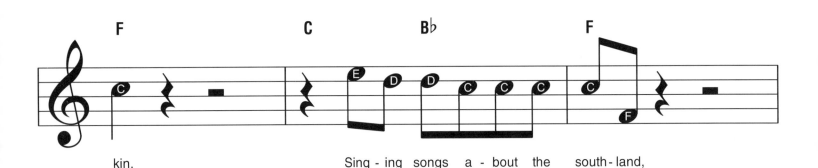

kin.   Sing - ing songs a - bout the south - land,

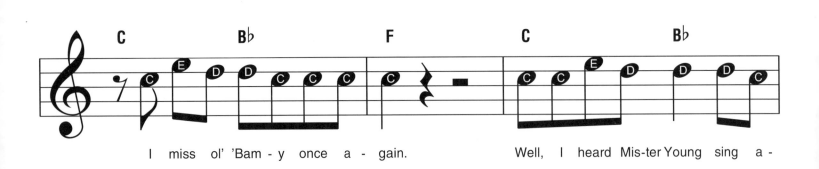

I miss ol' 'Bam - y once a - gain.   Well, I heard Mis-ter Young sing a -

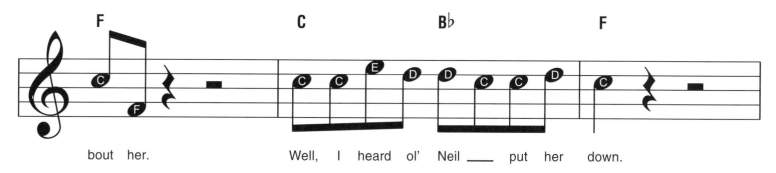

bout her.   Well, I heard ol' Neil ___ put her down.

Well, I hope Neil Young will re - mem - ber   a south-ern man don't need him a-

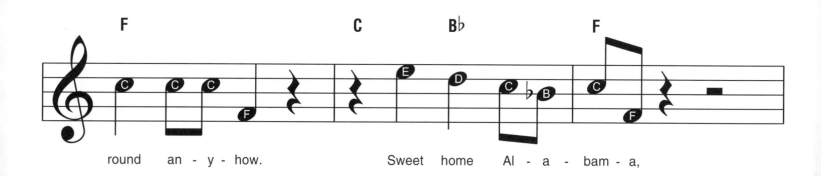

round an - y - how.   Sweet home Al - a - bam - a,

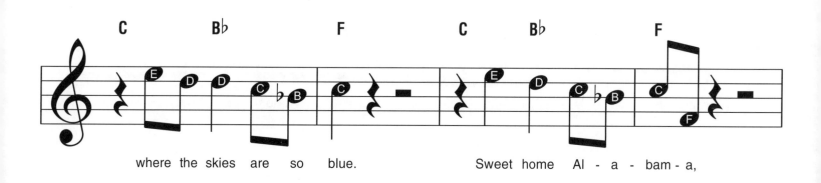

where the skies are so blue.   Sweet home Al - a - bam - a,

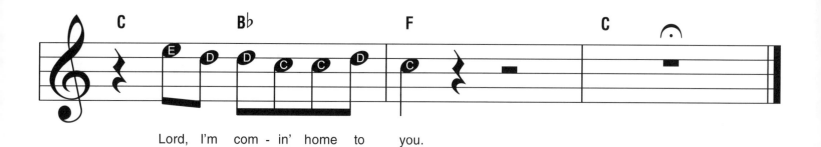

Lord, I'm com - in' home to you.

Takin' Care of Business

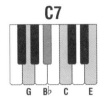
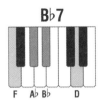
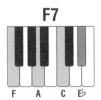

Words and Music by
Randy Bachman

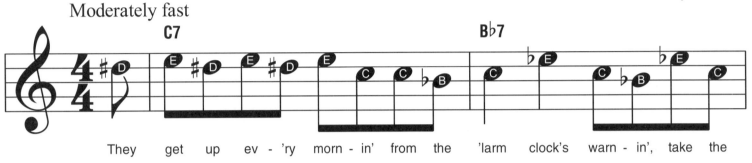

They get up ev-'ry morn-in' from the 'larm clock's warn-in', take the

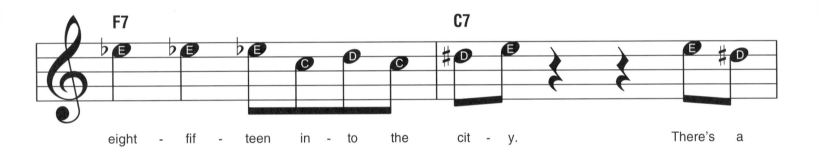

eight - fif - teen in - to the cit - y. There's a

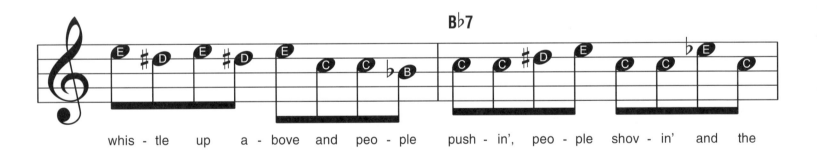

whis - tle up a - bove and peo - ple push-in', peo - ple shov-in' and the

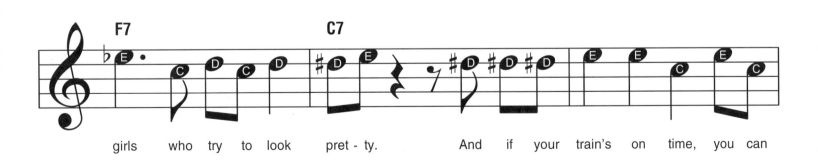

girls who try to look pret - ty. And if your train's on time, you can

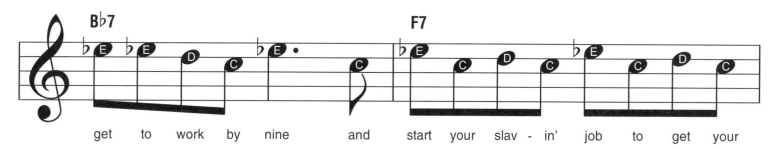

get to work by nine   and start your slav - in' job to get your

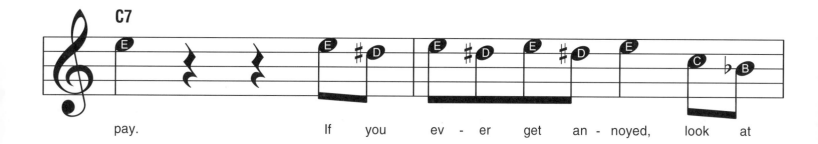

pay.   If you ev - er get an - noyed, look at

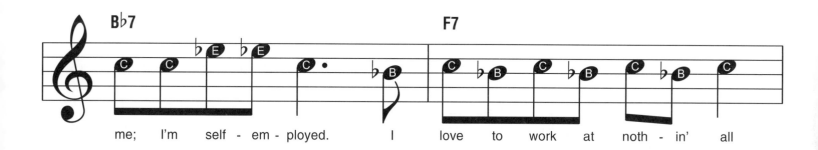

me; I'm self - em - ployed.   I love to work at noth - in' all

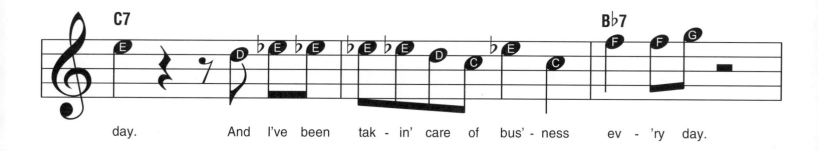

day.   And I've been tak - in' care of bus' - ness ev - 'ry day.

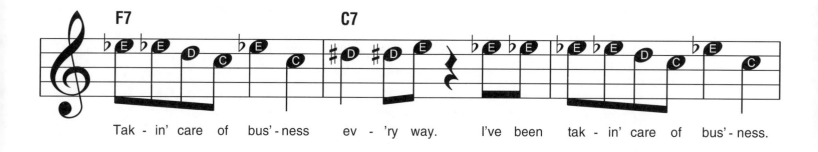

Tak - in' care of bus' - ness ev - 'ry way.   I've been tak - in' care of bus' - ness.

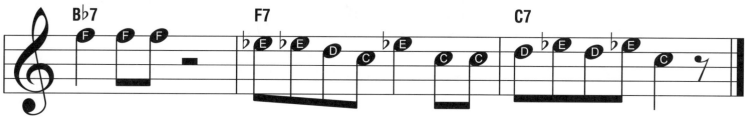

It's all mine.   Tak - in' care of bus' - ness and work - in' o - ver - time.

Time for Me to Fly

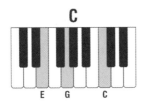
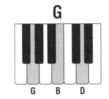
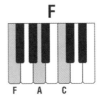

Words and Music by
Kevin Cronin

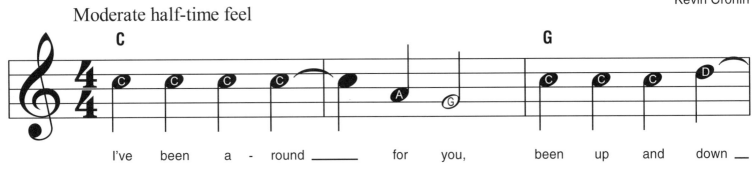

I've been a - round _____ for you, been up and down _____

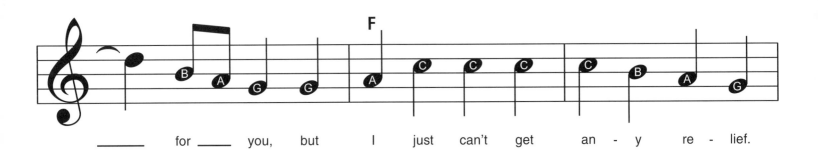

_____ for _____ you, but I just can't get an - y re - lief.

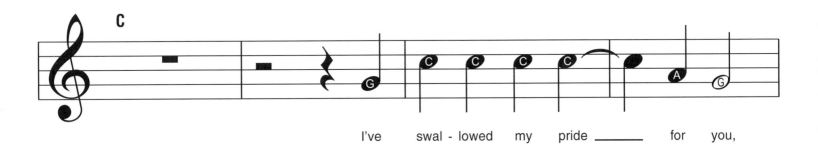

I've swal - lowed my pride _____ for you,

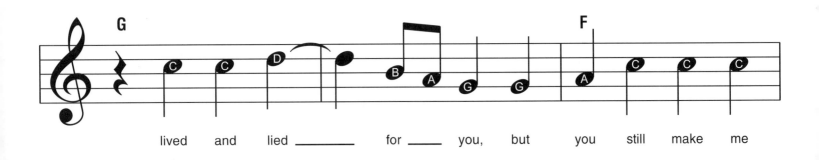

lived and lied _____ for _____ you, but you still make me

Turn Me Loose

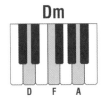
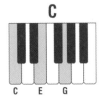

Words and Music by Paul Dean
and Duke Reno

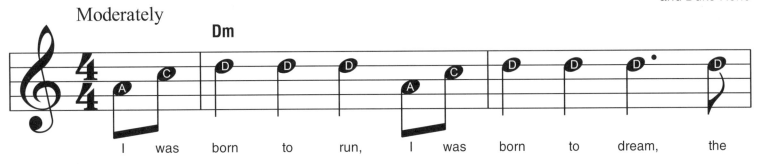

I was born to run, I was born to dream, the

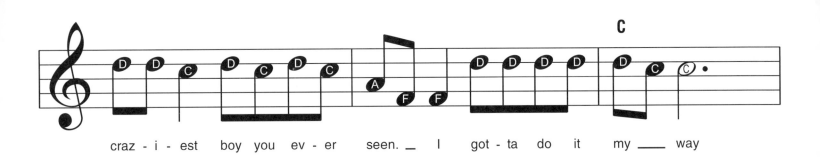

craz - i - est boy you ev - er seen. _ I got - ta do it my ___ way

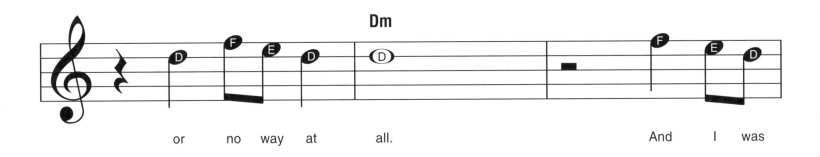

or no way at all. And I was

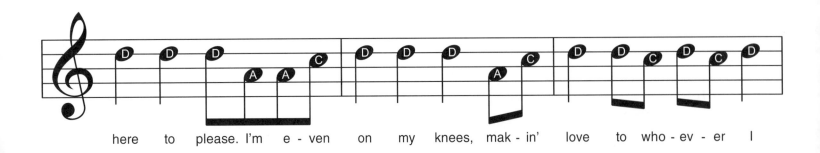

here to please. I'm e - ven on my knees, mak - in' love to who - ev - er I

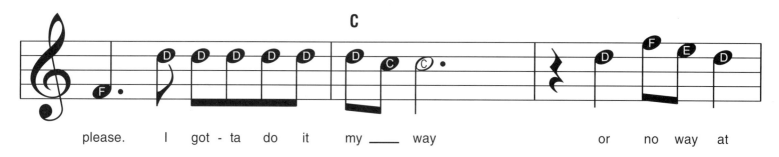

please. I got - ta do it my ___ way   or no way at

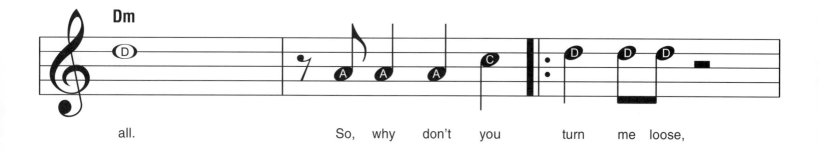

all.   So, why don't you   turn me loose,

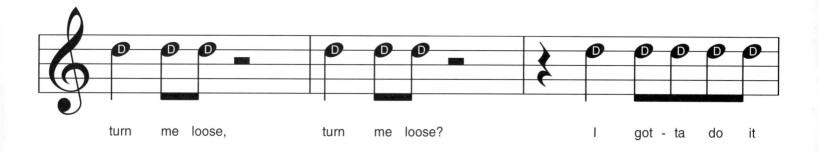

turn me loose,   turn me loose?   I got - ta do it

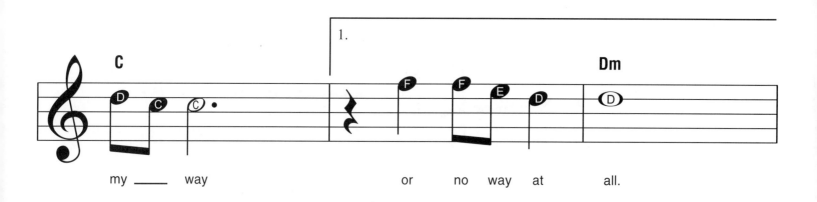

my ___ way   or no way at   all.

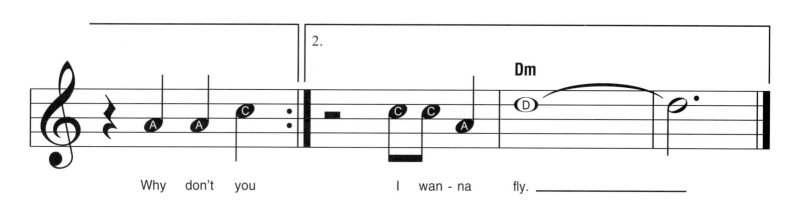

Why don't you   I wan - na   fly. _____

Walk This Way

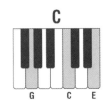
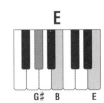
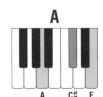

Words and Music by Steven Tyler
and Joe Perry

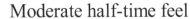

Moderate half-time feel

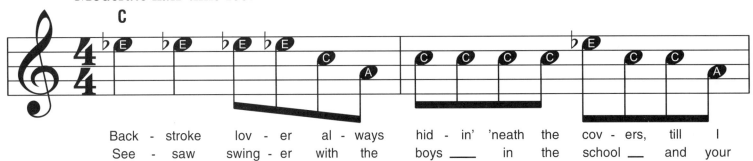

Back - stroke lov - er al - ways hid - in' 'neath the cov - ers, till I
See - saw swing - er with the boys ___ in the school ___ and your

talked to your dad - dy. He say, he said, "You ain't seen noth - in' till you're
feet fly - in' up in the air. Sing - in', "Hey did - dle did - dle" with your

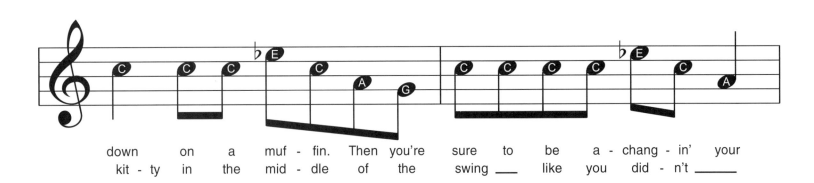

down on a muf - fin. Then you're sure to be a - chang - in' your
kit - ty in the mid - dle of the swing ___ like you did - n't ___

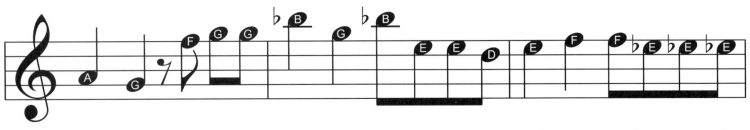

ways." ___ I met a cheer - lead - er, was a real young bleed - er. Oh, the
care. ____ So, I took a big chance ___ at the high school dance ___ with a

times I could rem - i - nisce. 'Cause the best things of lov - in' with her
mis - sy who was read-y to play. Was it me she was fool - in'? 'Cause she

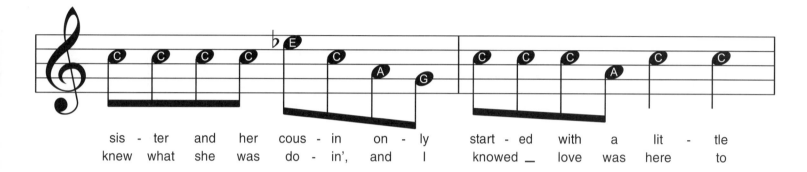

sis - ter and her cous - in on - ly start - ed with a lit - tle
knew what she was do - in', and I knowed __ love was here to

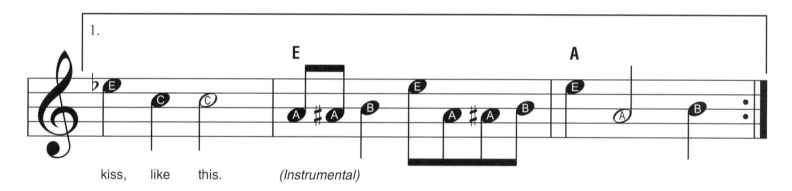

kiss, like this. (Instrumental)

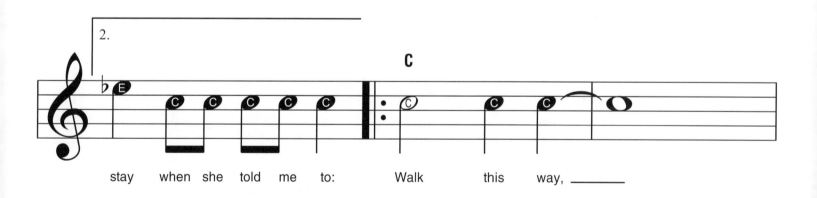

stay when she told me to: Walk this way, _____

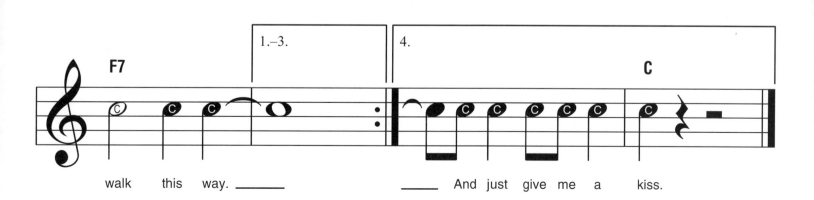

walk this way. _____   _____ And just give me a kiss.

Wanted Dead or Alive

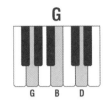
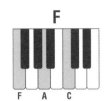
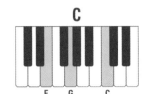
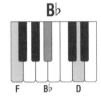

Words and Music by Jon Bon Jovi
and Richie Sambora

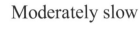

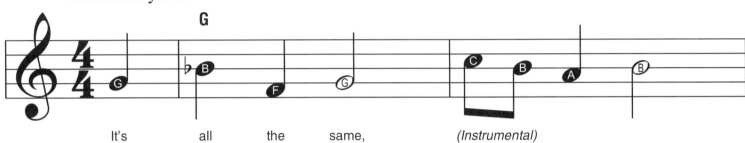

It's all the same, (Instrumental)

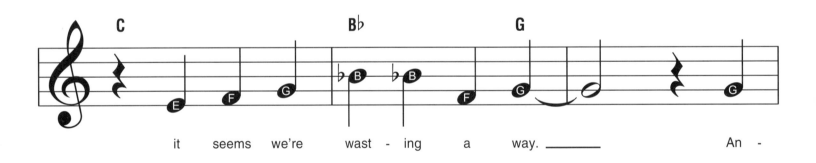

on - ly the names will change. _____ Ev - 'ry day

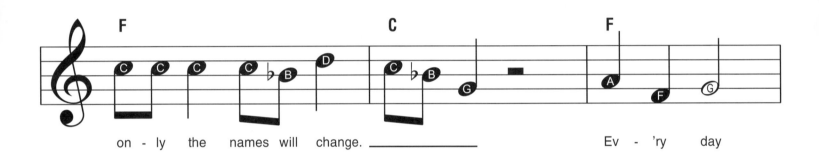

it seems we're wast - ing a way. _____ An -

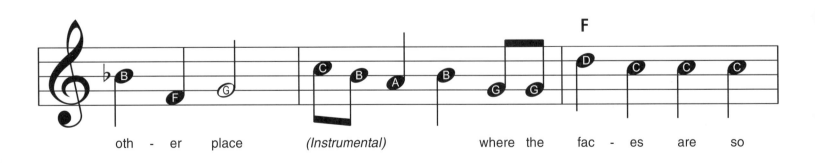

oth - er place (Instrumental) where the fac - es are so

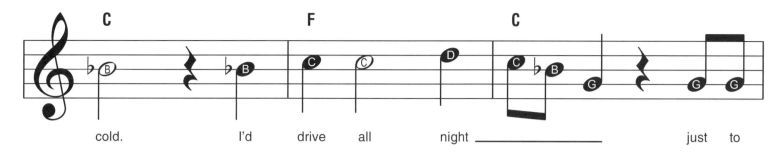

cold.   I'd   drive   all   night _____   just   to

get   back ____ home. ____   I'm   a   cow - boy,

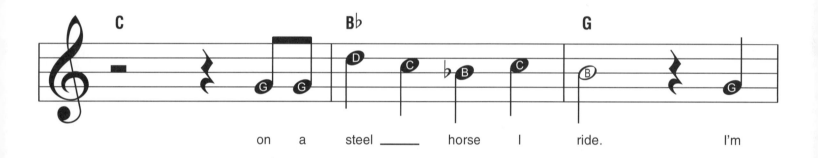

on   a   steel ____ horse   I   ride.   I'm

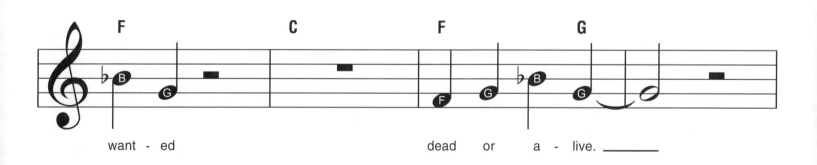

want - ed   dead   or   a - live. _____

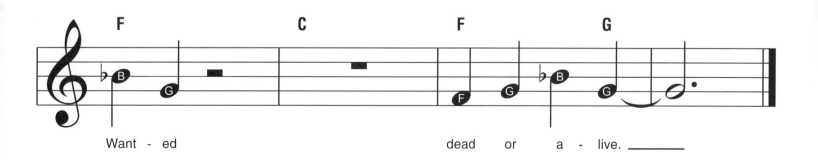

Want - ed   dead   or   a - live. _____

We Are the Champions

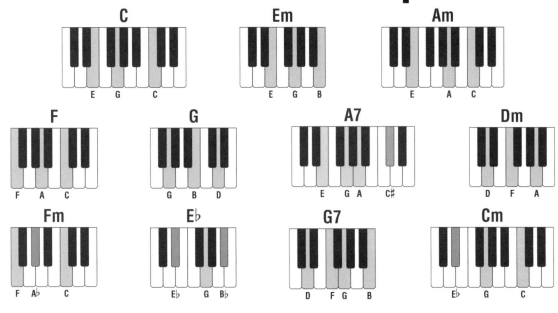

Words and Music by
Freddie Mercury

Moderately slow, in 1

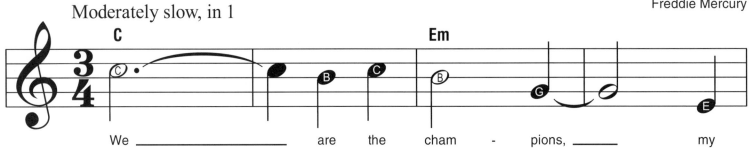

We _____ are the cham - pions, _____ my

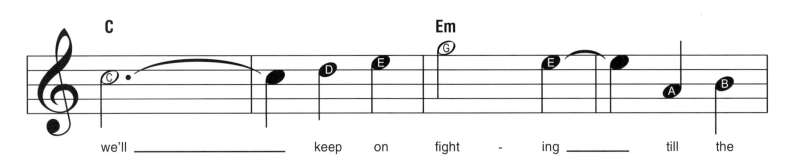

friend. _____ And

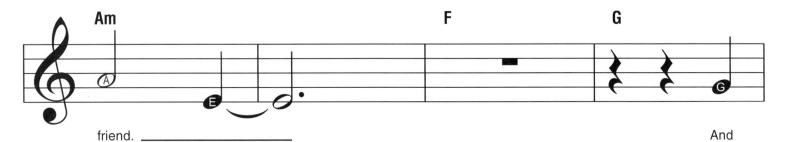

we'll _____ keep on fight - ing _____ till the

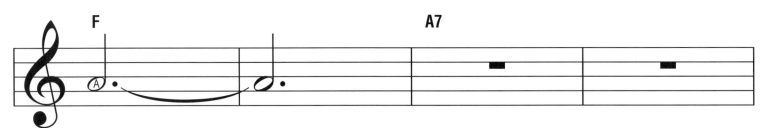

end. _____

Wish You Were Here

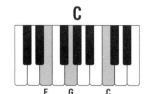 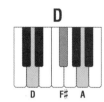 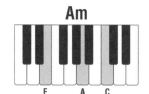 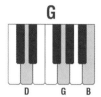 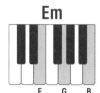

Words and Music by Roger Waters
and David Gilmour

Moderately

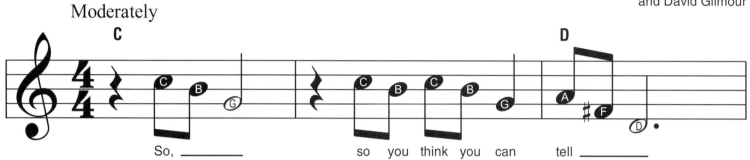

So, _____ so you think you can tell _____

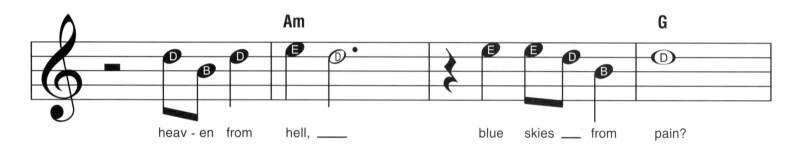

heav - en from hell, ____ blue skies ___ from pain?

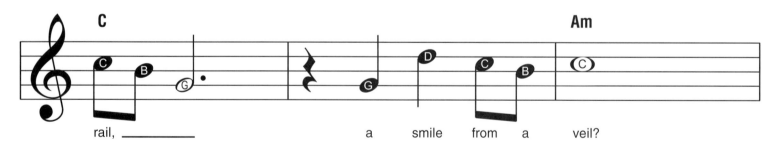

Can you tell a green __ field _____ from a cold, steel

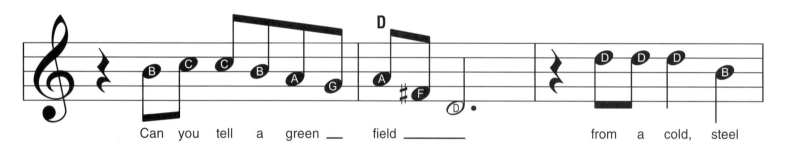

rail, _____ a smile from a veil?

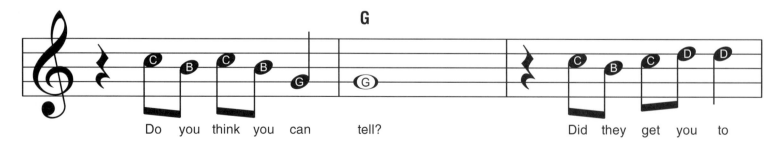

Do you think you can tell? Did they get you to

Won't Get Fooled Again

 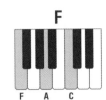 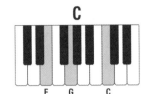 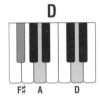

Words and Music by
Peter Townshend

Moderately fast

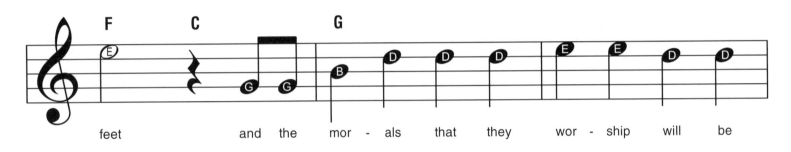

We'll be fight - ing in the streets with our chil - dren at our

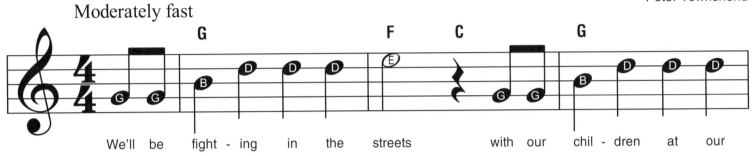

feet and the mor - als that they wor - ship will be

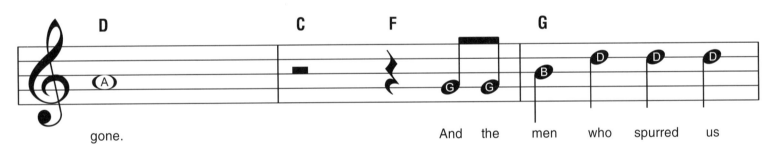

gone. And the men who spurred us

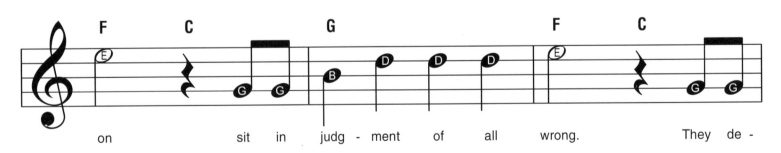

on sit in judg - ment of all wrong. They de -

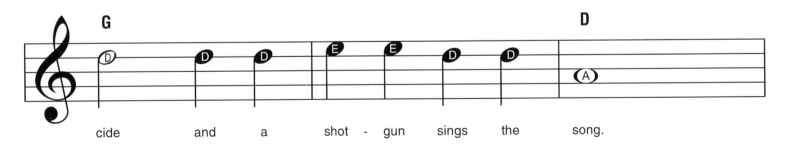

cide and a shot - gun sings the song.

115

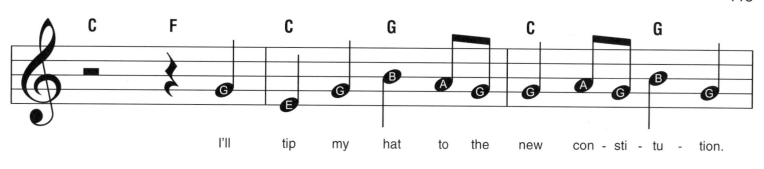

I'll tip my hat to the new con - sti - tu - tion.

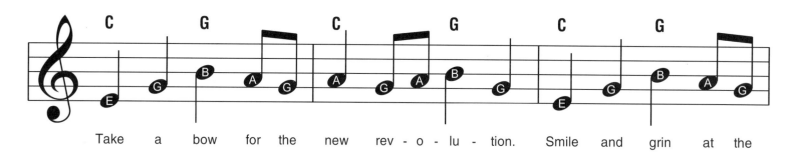

Take a bow for the new rev - o - lu - tion. Smile and grin at the

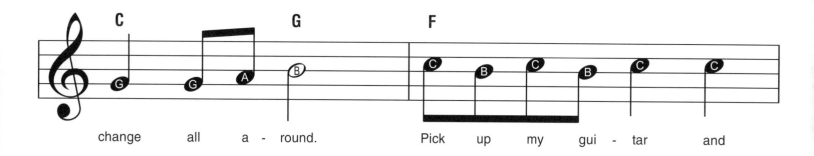

change all a - round. Pick up my gui - tar and

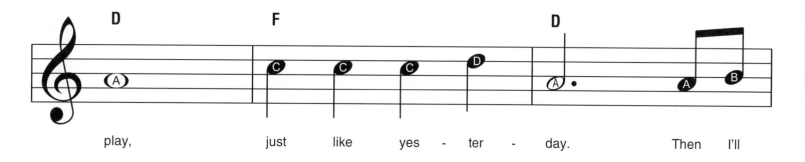

play, just like yes - ter - day. Then I'll

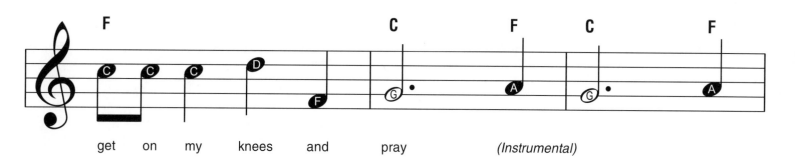

get on my knees and pray (Instrumental)

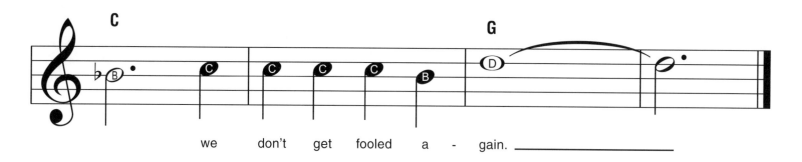

we don't get fooled a - gain.

Working for the Weekend

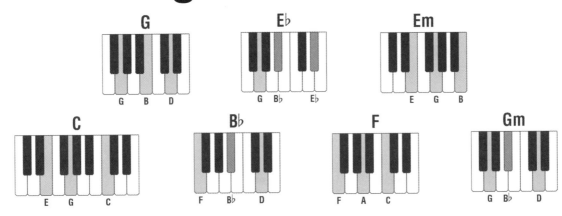

Words and Music by Paul Dean,
Matthew Frenette and Michael Reno

Moderately fast

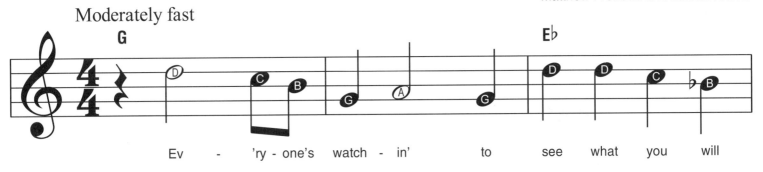

Ev - 'ry-one's watch - in' to see what you will

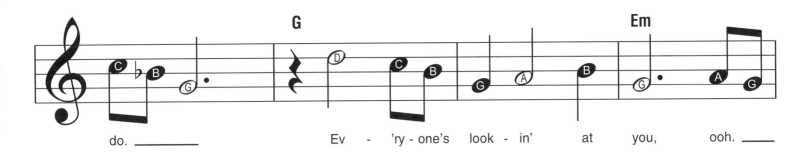

do. _____ Ev - 'ry-one's look - in' at you, ooh. ____

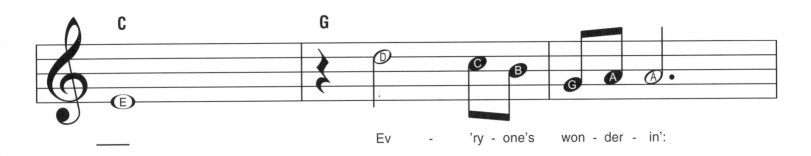

_____ Ev - 'ry-one's won - der - in':

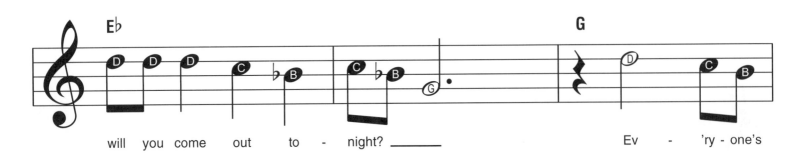

will you come out to - night? _____ Ev - 'ry-one's

You Really Got Me

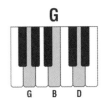
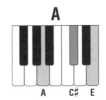
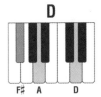

Words and Music by
Ray Davies

Moderately fast

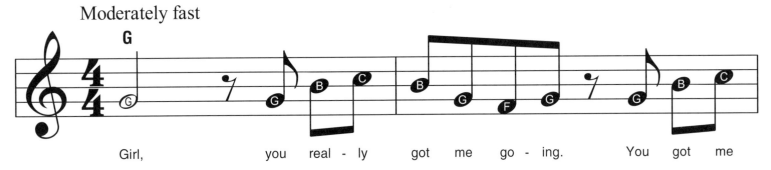

Girl, you real - ly got me go - ing. You got me

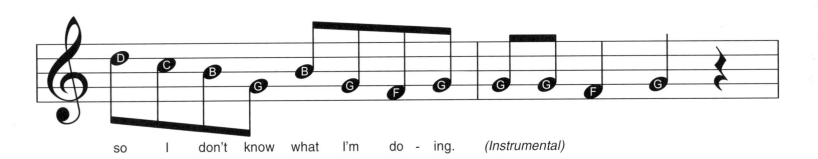

so I don't know what I'm do - ing. (Instrumental)

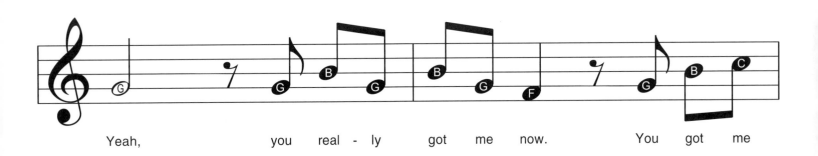

Yeah, you real - ly got me now. You got me

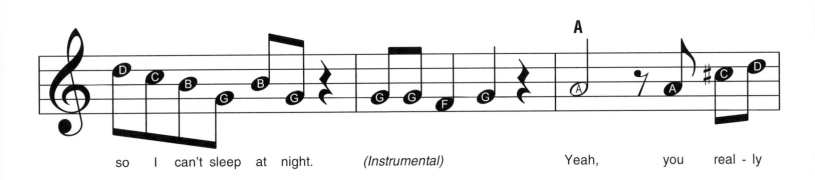

so I can't sleep at night. (Instrumental) Yeah, you real - ly

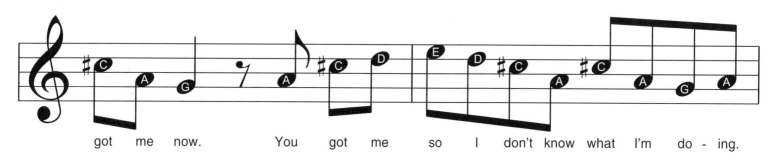

got me now. You got me so I don't know what I'm do - ing.

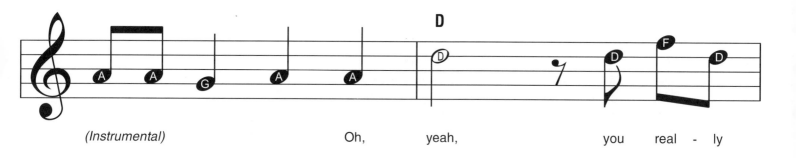

(Instrumental)   Oh,   yeah,   you real - ly

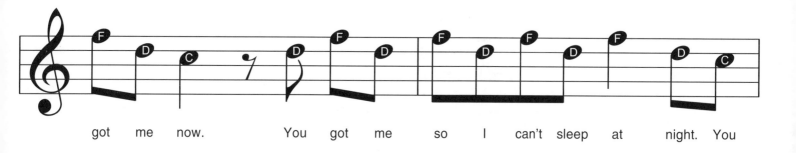

got me now. You got me so I can't sleep at night. You

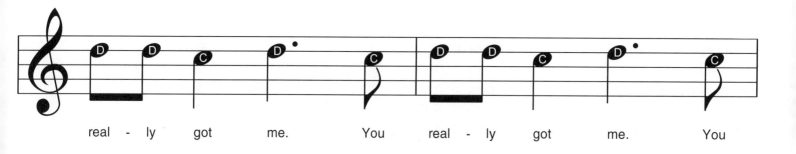

real - ly got me. You real - ly got me. You

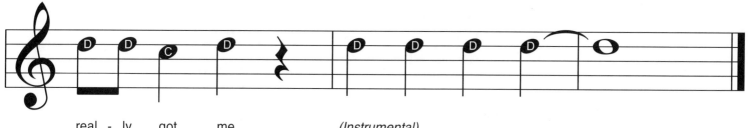

real - ly got me. *(Instrumental)*

SUPER EASY SONGBOOK

It's super easy! This series features accessible arrangements for piano, with simple right-hand melody, letter names inside each note, and basic left-hand chord diagrams. Perfect for players of all ages!

THE BEATLES
00198161 60 songs......................$15.99

BEAUTIFUL BALLADS
00385162 50 songs......................$14.99

BEETHOVEN
00345533 21 selections...............$9.99

BEST SONGS EVER
00329877 60 songs......................$16.99

BROADWAY
00193871 60 songs......................$15.99

JOHNNY CASH
00287524 20 songs......................$9.99

CHART HITS
00380277 24 songs......................$12.99

CHRISTMAS CAROLS
00277955 60 songs......................$15.99

CHRISTMAS SONGS
00236850 60 songs......................$15.99

CHRISTMAS SONGS WITH 3 CHORDS
00367423 30 songs......................$10.99

CLASSIC ROCK
00287526 60 songs......................$15.99

CLASSICAL
00194693 60 selections.............$15.99

COUNTRY
00285257 60 songs......................$15.99

DISNEY
00199558 60 songs......................$15.99

BOB DYLAN
00364487 22 songs......................$12.99

BILLIE EILISH
00346515 22 songs......................$10.99

FOLKSONGS
00381031 60 songs......................$15.99

FOUR CHORD SONGS
00249533 60 songs......................$15.99

FROZEN COLLECTION
00334069 14 songs......................$10.99

GEORGE GERSHWIN
00345536 22 songs......................$9.99

GOSPEL
00285256 60 songs......................$15.99

HIT SONGS
00194367 60 songs......................$16.99

HYMNS
00194659 60 songs......................$15.99

JAZZ STANDARDS
00233687 60 songs......................$15.99

BILLY JOEL
00329996 22 songs......................$10.99

ELTON JOHN
00298762 22 songs......................$10.99

KIDS' SONGS
00198009 60 songs......................$15.99

LEAN ON ME
00350593 22 songs......................$9.99

THE LION KING
00303511 9 songs........................$9.99

ANDREW LLOYD WEBBER
00249580 48 songs......................$19.99

MOVIE SONGS
00233670 60 songs......................$15.99

PEACEFUL MELODIES
00367880 60 songs......................$16.99

POP SONGS FOR KIDS
00346809 60 songs......................$16.99

POP STANDARDS
00233770 60 songs......................$16.99

QUEEN
00294889 20 songs......................$10.99

ED SHEERAN
00287525 20 songs......................$9.99

SIMPLE SONGS
00329906 60 songs......................$15.99

STAR WARS (EPISODES I-IX)
00345560 17 songs......................$10.99

TAYLOR SWIFT
1192568 30 songs........................$14.99

THREE CHORD SONGS
00249664 60 songs......................$15.99

TOP HITS
00300405 22 songs......................$10.99

WORSHIP
00294871 60 songs......................$15.99

Disney characters and artwork TM & © 2021 Disney

HAL•LEONARD®
www.halleonard.com